PRODUCT MASTERY

Geoff Watts

PRODUCT MASTERY

From Good to Great Product Ownership

Published February 2017

Edited by Rebecca Traeger

Design and illustrations by Ole H. Størksen

Printed by Amazon Createspace

First Edition Published 2017 by Inspect & Adapt Ltd

96 Redgrove Park, Cheltenham, Glos, GL51 6QZ

ISBN: 978-1540562548

Dedicated to

Jean Tabaka

Quite possibly the best human being I ever met. An inspiration and role model who, among other things pushed and supported me to start writing.

We miss you.

Table of Contents

Foreword – Jeff Sutherland

In 1994, the first Scrum team accelerated 400% in their third sprint. We had committed to ship the first release of a new product in Sprint 6. As acting Product Owner, I had enough product backlog for three sprints, now I needed enough product backlog for 12 sprints. It wasn't possible without a full time, great Product Owner!

I went to Product Marketing and told them I needed the best person in the company. His name was Don Roedner and he delivered Object Studio on time. Computer World reported it was the best product of its type they had ever seen. Today, over 20 years later, CINCOM reports the product is still profitable with a growing revenue and user base.

Don proved it is possible for a great Product Owner to deliver the best product of its type that the world has ever seen in less than six months.

You are about to read how Geoff believes a great Product Owner needs to be **Decisive, Ruthless, Informed, Versatile, Empowering, and Negotiable.** I consider Don to be a great Product Owner and while reading Geoff's book I looked back at how the characteristics he writes about mapped to Don.

Don chose to spend a lot of time with customers, going to conferences, looking at competitors' products yet he insisted on remaining available to the developers and spent half of his time with the team. He was the most informed person in the company about the product space and this was essential to his and the product's success.

Don knew that he would be measured by the greatness of the product when it was reviewed by Computer World and so he was **ruthless** in his prioritization of the product backlog. He was accountable, and he was **empowered** to make the necessary decisions to be successful; and boy was he **decisive**! He had many stakeholders to work with and his **negotiation** skills were a huge factor.

When thinking back to that very first Scrum team, I can't help but recall another of Don's characteristics that stood out which was his ability and willingness to challenge them to greatness and **empowering** them to own how to build the product.

Product Mastery is a great book to read if you want to understand how a great Product Owner works. Whether you are hiring a Product Owner or want to be a great Product Owner, the insights that Geoff Watts shares in this book should be your guide.

Jeff Sutherland
Co-Creator of Scrum
MIT Cambridge Innovation Center 2017
Author of *Scrum: The Art of Doing Twice the Work in Half the Time*

Foreword by Roman Pichler

Product owners are privileged to look after products, shape and progress them, and maximise the benefits they create for the users and for the business. At the same time, being a product owner is very challenging: product owners have a broad range of responsibilities and rely on a diverse group of people to help them make their product a success. But they have little or no authority over the development team and the stakeholders.

Being a successful product owner requires more than hard skills, such as being able to define the product strategy, create an actionable product roadmap, and prioritise the product backlog. It requires strong soft skills, including communication, stakeholder management, and decision-making. These not only require time and dedication to develop, but there is little advice available for product people to help them strengthen their soft skills. Luckily, this book fills the gap.

Geoff Watts draws on his wealth of knowledge and experience as a qualified coach, helping product owners develop and grow. Geoff has done a great job at distilling the soft skills product owners need to succeed. He discusses some of the traits that can prevent product people from doing a great job, such as procrastinating decisions out of fear of failure or perfectionism, and he explains how to overcome them.

His new book is packed with practical advice and I hope you will find it helpful to advance your skills and become a truly great product owner.

Roman Pichler
Author of *Strategize and Agile Product Management with Scrum*

Introduction to DRIVEN Product Ownership

For many years, people told me I should write a book but I laughed off their suggestions, partly because I didn't think I was capable or worthy, partly because I didn't think I had enough content and partly because I was daunted by the prospect.

Eventually, after coaching many people to challenge their perceptions of what was possible for them, I decided to walk the talk myself and did it. After a great deal of effort, I published my first book, *Scrum Mastery*, and I'm so glad I did.

While writing *Scrum Mastery*, I tackled my doubts through adopting an agile approach to the delivery of the book. I came up with a vision for it and tested it with the market—did people out there find the concept of the book attractive? I wrote a chapter and published it as a blog post, inviting feedback. Taking that feedback into account, I wrote another potential chapter, published it as a blog post and invited feedback on the new chapter.

Each step of the way I further validated my idea and got steadily closer to the goal, while simultaneously increasing my confidence in my ability to write (so much so that I later co-wrote and published a second book, *The Coach's Casebook*). The vision for *Scrum Mastery* remained relatively stable but the solution changed quite dramatically as it evolved, based both on the feedback I received and also on the evolution of my ideas throughout the writing process.

The response I have received since publishing *Scrum Mastery* has been wonderful. ScrumMasters have repeatedly told me how useful it has been in their day-to-day work. They have shared with me that Scrum has improved in their organisations since reading the book and that their teams have been more productive as a result. This is exactly what I was hoping for. Even so, these ScrumMasters aren't completely happy.

"There's no point in being an effective ScrumMaster," they tell me, "if the product owner doesn't also know how to do their job."

The product owner job is perhaps the most demanding role in terms of responsibilities and daily duties. The number one difficulty cited by product owners is that there aren't enough hours in the day to be an agile product manager.

This book, then, focuses on product owners—who they are, what they are expected to do, what they need to do, and how they might go about doing it in order to be effective, get the most out of Scrum, and build the best products possible.

Product Owner or Product Manager?

In general, I'm not one to worry too much about labels or job titles. In my day-to-day work you will probably find me using the terms product owner and product manager relatively interchangeably. This is because I don't really care what the role is called as long as that person is doing the job well.

However, there is a certain amount of confusion about whether these two jobs are the same or not. In my opinion, one of the reasons that the product owner role is so difficult is because it comprises even more authority than the traditional product manager—and that was a difficult enough job anyway.

Extra responsibility doesn't necessarily make a job harder though; in fact it can make a job easier if it's coupled with the necessary authority, skills and mindset to execute that responsibility. Scrum intends to offer the product owner that authority but it's not all about power.

Agile product management requires time, experience, gut instinct, self-confidence, humility, independence and collaboration skills, among other things.

For the purposes of this book, and for consistency, I will use the term product owner but if you find yourself in a role with the title product manager I believe what I have to say is equally valuable to you.

Good and Great

Those of you who have read *Scrum Mastery* will be familiar with my approach of describing the differences between what good behaviour is and what great behaviour is. Everything I describe in these books is positive as I have met very few people who act with the intention of deliberately messing things up.

This is in the spirit of the agile manifesto which describes valuing certain behaviours *over* others not instead of. If you think that the great behaviours are out of your reach right now, that's OK. Good enough is good enough. But always strive to improve. That is the mantra of the product owner anyway.

What Is a Great Product Owner?

I have identified a number of traits of successful product owners over the years; the best ones tend to have a number of common traits. For ease of organisation, and because everyone finds acronyms easier to remember, I have described the traits of a great product owner in terms of being DRIVEN.

Decisive:	Willing and able to make decisions with incomplete information, and to allow others to make decisions too
Ruthless:	Maintaining a relentless drive to maximise value and minimise risk while staying focused on the vision
Informed:	Cultivating a voracious appetite to know the most possible about your product's domain while being prepared to act with incomplete information
Versatile:	Being responsive to changing circumstances, both in terms of product development techniques and also leadership style
Empowering:	Creating a sense of shared ownership amongst all stakeholders and bringing people along with you on the journey
Negotiable:	Having faith in one's vision while also being open to feedback and change

In each section you will find a story or two that illustrate these characteristics as well as some theoretical explanation and self-reflection questions aimed at helping you find ways to develop in that area. I begin with Decisive and a story about a product owner whose product ultimately failed, at least in part because he couldn't make up his mind.

DRIVEN

Decisive

"Nothing is more difficult, and therefore more precious,
than to be able to decide."
Napoleon Bonaparte

Perhaps one of the most difficult aspects of being a DRIVEN product owner is learning how to be decisive in the face of incomplete information or conflicting priorities. When decisions are difficult it's tempting to put them off—to do a bit more research or talk to just a few more people first. It's equally tempting to avoid making a decision at all—promising instead to give everyone everything they want. The result, as you can probably guess, is that nothing of value is actually delivered.

Good product owners overcome these tendencies first by understanding the reasons behind their inaction and then by taking concrete steps to make progress without compromising the future. In the face of fear and uncertainty, great product owners are DRIVEN to make a decision and move forward.

Ensuring that the right decision is made at the right time by the right people requires a great deal of courage, confidence, self-awareness and humility. In the following story and discussions we will see how decisive product owners need to be brave and trust themselves—and others—to make decisions with incomplete information, recognizing both what they know and what they don't know. We'll also discuss several strategies to help make the overall decision-making process easier, cheaper and more reversible.

*We still don't have a comprehensive
evaluation of everything that's available—
and I don't think we ever will.*

Delay and Decide

Good product owners delay when they can.
Great product owners decide when they must.

Kenny was a Studio Director for a video game development company that had won many prestigious awards and received rave reviews for its previous games, but was struggling to release its newest game. After nine months in research and development, the development team were finally ready to begin. The long delay, however, had spooked the company's financial backers, who were getting twitchy. Kenny's boss, Donald, who was getting most of the pressure from the backers, dropped by Kenny's office to check on progress. One of the first questions he asked was why the R&D was taking so long.

"We never intended to take nine months," Kenny admitted. "What we are doing is equivalent to writing a whole new operating system, so we knew we had to research a whole load of new technologies. We needed to make sure we picked the best one, so we budgeted three to four months to get it right. But by the time we were ready to report our findings, new technologies had emerged, so we scheduled another couple of months to evaluate those."

"I think I see where this is going," Donald said. "You just kept chasing your tail because there was always something new out there that might be better than what you had already looked at?"

"Exactly," Kenny said. "In truth, we could probably have created a couple of small games in the time that we've spent researching. What's worse is that even after all of this time, we still don't have a comprehensive evaluation of everything that's available—and I don't think we ever will."

Kenny and Donald discussed how this was far from a dead end. "You have enough research to make a decision," Donald explained. "You just need to be brave and choose the best solution available to you today."

Kenny agreed. Over the next few days, he and the team chose the technology they thought was the best bet and moved on to planning the actual game. In planning, though, Kenny once again demonstrated the same mindset that had driven his desire to have a comprehensive analysis of the technology options.

After meeting with the stakeholders, Kenny created a list of requirements that, when the team estimated them, turned out to be somewhere in the region of three years work. This wouldn't have been a problem if the stakeholders had agreed to allow the team to develop and deliver the product iteratively and incrementally. The stakeholders, however, were firmly of the opinion that the game could not be released in stages without undermining the unique selling points of the game: the unlimited size of the world that the player was part of and the multiple, long-term connectivity options. And Kenny was inclined to agree.

Though the team and Kenny spent many hours looking at ways of slicing the game up so that it could be delivered incrementally, Kenny ultimately decided it had to be "all or nothing." Even though, on some level, they all understood the need to get something valuable to market, Kenny and the stakeholders couldn't let go of the big picture vision enough to do that.

A few months later the financial backers decided to pull the funding for the game. Not long afterwards, the once successful company shut its doors forever.

Decide What's Making the Decision Difficult

We've all been in a similar circumstance to Kenny at one time or another, where we simply cannot make up our minds. In Kenny's case, his inability to make a decision ultimately put him (and everyone else at his company) out of work. The question is, why is decision making sometimes so hard? In my book, *The Coach's Casebook*, I write about the personality traits and traps that can hold people back in their personal and professional lives, and some strategies to overcome them. I share some of that insight throughout this book to help explain what might be going on beneath the surface that might make one or more of the DRIVEN traits more difficult to achieve at first. Often, when someone is indecisive, they are struggling against a tendency to procrastinate. That was certainly the case with Kenny.

Oddly enough, when it comes to decision making, some procrastination can be helpful. In uncertain environments it can be incredibly valuable to adopt the general principle of delaying as long as possible in order to allow yourself maximum time to gather enough data to make the best decision. An added benefit of this is that sometimes, by not making a decision right away, the problem may just disappear.

In the article, *"Waiting Game: What Tennis Teaches Us,"* social scientist and author Frank Partnoy explains how all decisions, from tennis players returning a serve to Wall Street traders executing a trade, can and often do benefit from being made at the last possible moment:

"During superfast reactions, the best-performing experts instinctively know when to pause, if only for a split-second. The same is true over longer periods: some of us are better at understanding when to take a few extra seconds to deliver the punch line of a joke, or when we should wait a full hour before making a judgment about another person. Part of this skill is gut instinct, and part of it is analytical" *(2011, para. 3).*

In the same article, Partnoy asserts that the best players at returning serves actually delay their return longer. They train to increase their swing speed so that they are able to use more time watching the ball and to delay making the decision until a more optimal time. As Partnoy says, these players "procrastinate—at the speed of light" *(para. 2).*

The problem is, we seldom procrastinate at the speed of light. Instead, as the story about Kenny illustrates all too clearly, what starts out as a valuable delay to gather data can quickly become costly and paralysing procrastination. This level of procrastination is caused by a range of issues, from simple to complex. Some of the issues Kenny seemed to struggle with include:

- Overwhelming amount of options or information
- Fear of failure
- Perfectionism
- Lack of assertiveness

Remember that in the beginning of the story, Kenny struggled to choose a technology. In fact, he spent nine long months researching technology options only to emerge with no clear winner. Kenny said the reason he couldn't decide was there were just too many options to explore, and every time he thought he had settled on one, a new possibility would become available.

This inability to make a decision when faced with too many choices was famously studied by Sheena Iyengar and Mark Lepper. In their 2000 paper, *"When Choice is Demotivating: Can One Desire Too Much of a Good Thing?"* they found that when presented with 6 different kinds of jam, 30 percent of people ultimately bought one of the jams. However, when presented with 24 types of jam, an incredible 97 percent of people ended up buying nothing. Iyenger and Lepper concluded that too many options made decision making more difficult.

Though later studies have attempted to determine whether the problem is too many options or too much information, the effect remains the same. Decisions can be much more difficult when you have many similar options to choose from and not much to distinguish them.

Could you reduce the number of options you are considering?

Would this make it easier for you to decide?

In the story, Kenny seems to struggle with more than just an over-abundance of options, though. His fear of making the wrong choice or even a suboptimal one might point to either a fear of failure or to perfectionism. As I discuss more fully in *The Coach's Casebook*, people who procrastinate out of a fear of failure may be unconsciously changing the question from "Am I able to do this?" to "Am I able to do this with very little time." In other words, it isn't that they can't do something—it is just that they can't do it in such a limited amount of time. No one, including themselves, can judge them harshly for being unable to perform given the time constraints! Perfectionists, have a similar problem, in that they fear being wrong so strongly that they simply avoid choosing in order to avoid judgement.

What are you assuming will happen if your decision turns out to be incorrect?

Are those assumptions valid?

Later in the story, when Kenny and the stakeholders ultimately sink the project because they cannot choose a smaller slice of the game to develop, Kenny seems to demonstrate a lack of assertiveness (perhaps due to an overdone tendency to please others). On the more technical side of things, Kenny also shows a lack of understanding of the value of incremental and iterative development in helping to make decisions.

Good product owners know that quickly delivering something that works and then learning from the feedback is the best way to ensure that the product is moving in the right direction. Great product owners are able to generate buy-in when stakeholders disagree and realise that not making a decision is still, in effect, making a decision—the decision not to act right now.

Decide When to Decide

Product owners must have the courage to make decisions with imperfect and incomplete information. Many decisions benefit greatly from diligent analysis and consideration. Great product owners, though, find ways to make quicker decisions safely—to do their research, consult with others, and hedge their bets where necessary.

When it comes to the timing of decisions, great product owners work toward two goals:

- Delay decisions until the last responsible moment
- Make it easier to make early decisions by reducing the cost of being wrong.

The last responsible moment is the time when the cost of not making a decision exceeds the cost of making a decision or, as Karl Scotland puts it, *"The Last Responsible Moment is just before the Cost of Delay outweighs the Benefit of Delay" (2010, para. 2)*. Kenny wasn't wrong to delay making a decision until he had evaluated the potential technology choices. After all, thinking about the future is a good thing. If we were to focus exclusively on the here and now, then we would be likely to end up with serious issues later.

For example, without some forethought, products might be misaligned with others in the portfolio or maintenance costs might skyrocket because of a lack of standardisation. However, with pressures on cycle times so high, and the life expectancies of products (and entire companies!) so low, the reality is that product owners must focus more on getting a working product to market than about future-proofing the design. In the story, Kenny went way past the point where the cost of delay (the loss of the financial backers) outweighed the benefit of that delay (future proofing the design). Eventually, he wisely took the advice of his boss and chose the best solution available at the time.

Even so, Kenny would have been much better off if he had found a way to reduce the cost of being wrong so that he could have made this choice much earlier. One bad decision, made early and discovered early through feedback, is relatively inexpensive to correct. Conversely, a bad decision made early and not delivered (and therefore not discovered) until the end of the project is extremely expensive to reverse. In their book *Lean Software Development: An Agile Toolkit,* Mary and Tom Poppendieck explain that this is because additional functionality and decisions have now been piled on top of that first bad decision, making the cost of change astronomical.

In situations where a number of viable options exist, one way to narrow down the possibilities is to allow the multiple options to progress concurrently for a set amount of time. This is called set-based decision making. Set-based decision making could involve prototyping various packaging designs and testing the market, A-B testing a new website design, or running two call-centre scripts in parallel and gathering feedback regarding which is the most effective. In Kenny's case, rather than simply have a pure research phase, Kenny could have allocated one month to choosing the two or three most likely technology candidates. Then, in the first iteration, he could have asked the team to develop the most important feature (or some small chunk of that feature) using each of the technologies.

At the end of the first iteration, not only would Kenny and the team have gathered more information about the technology choices, they also would have created something demonstrable for the financial backers and for gathering feedback. At that point, they might have been able to choose the best technology or they might have decided to do another test, but they could have continued to explore while creating real features.

In his 2011 TED Talk *"Trial, Error and the God Complex,"* economist Tim Harford explains how trial and error allowed Unilever to create a revolutionary new design for a nozzle in detergent manufacturing. The nozzle was designed by testing ten random variations, choosing the best of those, then testing ten more random variations of the chosen design, and so on. Not even the best designers at Unilever could explain why their final design worked, but it did.

While a trial-and-error approach may seem at first like an incredible waste (99 percent of those nozzle prototypes were in effect unsuccessful), when the answer is unknown and the cost of the wrong decision is high then concurrently pursuing multiple possible right answers for a few iterations ultimately reduces risk, negating the cost of the waste. Plus, working in an environment where experimentation is the norm helps reduce any fear associated with choosing the wrong path. As Edison once famously said, "I have not failed. I've just found 10,000 ways that won't work."

Going back to the story and Kenny, had he and the team taken a try-and-see approach, not only would they have something tangible to show for their research, but they also would have gained a much better idea of the advantages and disadvantages of the technologies if they had used them to develop some of the actual requirements of the game.

Great product owners know that reducing the consequences of making the wrong decision is a great supporting strategy to help them make early decisions, while still delaying unnecessary commitments.

> If you knew that it was impossible to make a perfect decision, how would that help you?

Decide Where to Focus First

The true death knell for Kenny's project came when he and the stakeholders failed to define a product that could be delivered quickly. Instead, they took an all-or-nothing approach to delivery. This meant that no portion of the product could be delivered until every desired feature was complete. Agile product owners have learned the hard way that they cannot afford to leave all of the delivery until the end of the project.

Instead, agile product owners start by taking their long list of must-have products and even longer list of must-have features and focusing first on the single most important product, and then on the single most important feature for that product. After implementing that first feature and receiving feedback, the product owner can approach the second most-important feature with more data and less uncertainty. Not only are more features delivered earlier using this method, but also each implemented feature further reduces the risk and uncertainty associated with the remaining features.

But how do agile product owners decide which product and which feature is most important? Most often, product owners try to make these decisions based on which features provide the most value. However, value is often subjective and can be an elusive thing to define. Numerous prioritisation strategies exist, with no "one size fits all" approach. As such, great product owners tend to adapt their prioritisation strategy to the context they are currently facing, with the goal of maximising value and reducing risk as early as possible.

As mentioned previously, product owners face huge time pressures. That's why, when looking at the concept of value, great product owners take into account not just revenue and profit but also cost and the cost of delay.

The following table lists three fictional products, with different timescales, costs, revenues and profits. I will use these projects to illustrate several prioritisation strategies that product owners might employ to determine which product to deliver first.

Product	Length	Cost	Projected Revenue	ROI	CD3
Blue	3 months	£8,000	£45,000	5.625	15.00
Green	4 months	£10,000	£75,000	7.500	18.75
Red	5 months	£20,000	£85,000	4.250	17.00

One strategy would be to prioritise the product that is quickest to complete. After all, this would be the fastest way to realise value. If **quick wins** are the priority, the product owner could choose to develop these products in the following order: Blue then Green then Red.

Another strategy would be to take the projects in order of the revenue they would yield. If **maximizing revenue** is the priority, the product owner could deliver the products in this order: Red then Green then Blue.

Perhaps profit is the driving factor. If so, the product owner could use a basic ROI calculation of Revenue/Cost to determine that the optimal delivery order in terms of **profit** is Green then Blue then Red.

Another factor to consider might be the cost of delay, or more precisely CD3. CD3 is the shorthand way of writing Cost of Delay Divided by Duration. CD3 has many other applications, but it's also a great tool to help product owners determine the relative value of competing products. In practice, Cost of Delay can be difficult to calculate as it may include many factors, including actual costs, opportunity costs, peak benefits, and the degree to which value decays over time. For simplicity's sake, I will just use the *projected revenue* figure in the table above as the Cost of Delay. If the product owner wants to focus on the product with the **highest CD3** first, then the products could be delivered in the order Green then Red then Blue.

These same approaches can also be used for prioritising feature delivery within product development efforts.

I hasten to emphasise that none of these prioritisation approaches is inherently right or wrong. Instead, the best strategy is the one that addresses the most pressing factor for the situation at hand. All product owners must act based on incomplete information and without a crystal ball. As such, it is often impossible to make a perfect decision. But by assessing the various facets of what makes a product or feature valuable, product owners can choose the most important product or feature with greater confidence, which—coupled with the iterative and incremental delivery of the high-priority features—makes even imperfect decisions far less costly and risky.

The different approaches above have the added benefit of allowing product owners to make conscious decisions about the possible economic trade-offs affecting their decisions, which in turn reduces the risk of the decisions negatively impacting their strategic goals.

Decide to Be Brave

Whatever the dilemma and no matter the strategy they choose to face it, great product owners are brave enough to actually *make a decision*. Then, once they make that decision, they stand by it, while also being prepared to adjust course based on what they learn.

Remember also that *not* making a decision is still a form of decision. And sometimes it's the right decision to make: Delaying unnecessary decisions in an uncertain world is often a very good strategy. It is important to keep in mind, however, that although good product owners delay some decisions until later, great product owners never shirk their decision-making responsibilities.

DRIVEN product owners manage to strike a balance between making quick decisions and delaying commitments. When they get stuck, they recognize and consciously choose to tackle whatever is undermining their ability to make a choice, whether that's a fear of failure, the desire to be perfect, too many options to choose from, a struggle with assertiveness, or something else.

Great product owners understand how crucial it is to ask other's advice.

Give and Take

Good product owners trust themselves
to make the tough calls.
Great product owners know when to call for help.

Good product owners know when to step up and make a decision for the good of the product. Great product owners also understand how crucial it is to ask the advice of others before making certain decisions, to sometimes let others make the decisions instead, and to generate buy in for decisions that are complex and affect multiple business units. Understanding this and doing it, however, are often two very different things.

For example, one of the most common reasons good product owners struggle to ask for help with decisions has to do with the Impostor Syndrome. Generally speaking, those who struggle with Impostor Syndrome believe that they are not as good as people think they are—that they are a fraud who will eventually be "found out". As I write in *The Coach's Casebook*, although Impostor Syndrome can be a component behind the success of many people, it is usually more damaging than it is helpful.

People with Impostor Syndrome face the following challenges:

- An inability to internalise accomplishments.
- A feeling that they are a fraud, that other people have an overinflated view of them.
- A belief that their successes can be attributed only to luck or being in the right place at the right time.
- A fear of being found out or labelled a fraud.
- A larger focus on what they can't do, rather than what they can do.

When you feel like an impostor, it can make it difficult not only to trust your own decisions but also to admit when you just don't know enough and need help to make a decision. After all, if you already feel like a fraud, owning up to your ignorance on a given topic will just amplify any feelings you might have of not being good enough, smart enough, or informed enough.

Decide to Believe in Yourself

Great product owners overcome this, first by recognising that Impostor Syndrome is incredibly common: in fact, my experience aligns with a *2014 report* by Margie Warrell that suggests up to 70 percent of people will experience this at some point, so they are not alone in feeling this way. Then they remind themselves of what they *do* know and what they are good at, appreciating that it is not rude, or arrogant, to internalise and own their successes and strengths.

Great product owners also realise that making products is a complex endeavor and that the chances of any single person knowing everything are slim. In Leonard Read's essay *I, pencil,* he quite eloquently makes the following statement about the pencil's supposed simplicity:

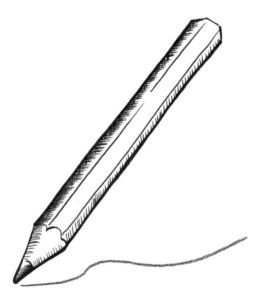

"Simple? Yet, not a single person on the face of this earth knows how to make me" (1999, RP. 5).

Internalising the truth that they are not expected to know everything helps great product owners forgive themselves for not being perfect—for not having all the answers—so that they can then feel confident and secure enough to ask for the advice and counsel of others. They know that admitting what they don't know will not make them look weak or foolish, but wise and strong.

As such, they rely on others for advice and recommendations when making difficult decisions. They understand when to make the tough calls themselves and when to delegate certain decisions to those with greater knowledge, be that the development team on how to build the product or subject matter experts with regards to functionality and usability.

 How many good decisions have you made that you haven't acknowledged?

Decide Not to Do It Alone

To help them make the many varied decisions about products and features, great product owners build comprehensive teams of subject-matter experts called product owner teams. They then consult with these teams on specific aspects where niche expertise is valuable. There are two types of product owner teams.

1. The scaled group of product owners on a product development effort with multiple development teams.
2. The cross-functional group of people whose collective expertise is needed to guide and support the leading of the product development effort.

Although both kinds of teams can be valuable, this chapter is concerned with the second type.

> Whose advice would be useful to include in your decision making process that you are currently shutting out?

Decide Who to Include

Great product owners know where knowledge resides and who to call on. They ask themselves the following questions:

- Who has information that would be useful in defining, prioritising, and understanding the features the product will need?
- Whose support might I need when considering the entire product development lifecycle?

Sometimes the answer to these questions is obvious. Product owners must be careful, though, if the decision about who to include seems too easy. It can be tempting for product owners to surround themselves only with those people they like—people who share their views and won't challenge them too much.

Great product owners know, however, that the best decisions take into account multiple viewpoints. They understand that people that disagree with them aren't sitting in judgement but instead are offering a valuable perspective. They create teams of allies and dissenters and give equal voice to both groups.

Practically speaking, every product owner team will be different depending on the context of the product in question, and might change over the life of the product development effort. With that being said, Figure D-1 shows the groups that are commonly represented in a product owner team:

Figure D-1. A product owner team represents the diverse interests associated with a product.

Decide What They Can Decide

The product owner team exists to support the product owner, so great product owners learn to trust their team's judgement and stand by the decisions the team is empowered to make. While their exact function will vary from team to team and probably week to week, typically the product owner team has the following responsibilities:

- Provide knowledge, advice, and counsel on priorities, risks, and dependencies.
- Feed requirements into the product backlog, possibly in the form of user stories.
- Offer feedback on development efforts at events such as the sprint review.
- Collaborate with the development team(s) in the role of subject-matter experts.
- Prepare downstream systems for the deliveries provided by the development team.

Each product owner team needs to determine the mechanics and logistics of their collaboration based on their circumstances but most of the effective product owner teams I have seen tend to collaborate at the following key times:

- At the beginning of the product development effort, when the product backlog is being formed and the initial plan is being pulled together.
- At least once or twice during each sprint to work through the questions or challenges arising that sprint.
- Once during the sprint to prepare the product backlog for the next sprint planning meeting. This is usually called a *backlog refinement workshop* or *backlog grooming workshop*.
- At the sprint review meeting to provide feedback on the latest iteration.

Though product owner teams can be an effective way of making the complicated job of the product owner doable, bear in mind that no matter how a decision is made, or by whom, the product owner will always retain accountability for it. For that reason, it's important that the product owner and the team develop a consistent decision-making strategy—and stick to it.

Decide How You Will Decide

One of the most important steps in creating an effective decision-making strategy is to prioritise the decisions, reserving more time for the decisions that are more important to get right or the ones that require greater buy in, and understanding when it is appropriate to delegate less important decisions to people with a better ability to make them. For example, a product owner might ask a member of the product owner team with marketing expertise to help determine the best set of beta users for a release.

Please don't misunderstand. I am not recommending that product owners hand off all responsibility to product owner teams or to a proxy. Product owners should only delegate decisions when it makes sense—they should make all crucial decisions personally, remembering that they retain accountability for every decision, no matter its priority. That's why knowing which decisions are crucial, and which can be delegated, is essential to an effective decision-making strategy.

Use a Decision-Making Matrix

I recommend that product owners use a decision-making matrix, such as the one shown here, to help them evaluate upcoming decisions. By assessing the complexity of the decision, the risk involved in getting that decision wrong, and the degree of buy-in needed, product owners can choose the right strategy for the situation.

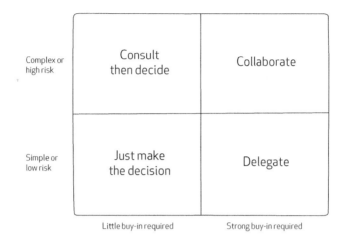

	Little buy-in required	Strong buy-in required
Complex or high risk	Consult then decide	Collaborate
Simple or low risk	Just make the decision	Delegate

Figure D-2. A decision-making matrix can help determine who should make a decision.

The first tactic is to identify the easy decisions—the ones that are low risk or low complexity and require little buy-in. Great product owners know how to identify simple decisions. They either make simple decisions quickly (when no one has a strong opinion either way) or they delegate these choices to someone else (when they desire increased stakeholder engagement and buy in).

For example, a product owner could decide the size and shape of the packaging for the product relatively quickly. However, if the product owner were to delegate responsibility for this decision to someone else, then that person suddenly has a much bigger stake in the product—and greater motivation to see that the product succeeds. In general, the more that people are involved in the decision-making process, the more engaged they are and the more bought-in they are to the decision.

Generating buy-in is equally important when product owners must rely on more than just their own authority for a course of action to be successful. For example, the product release date will likely affect many people. The more that each one of the affected parties has been included in the process of choosing a date, the more likely they are to ensure that the product releases on that date.

Because the release date affects so many people and has such an impact on the bottom line, it is arguably more critical and complex than deciding on the size and shape of the packaging. Therefore, most great product owners would typically adopt a strategy of collaboration rather than delegation when trying to choose the best release date. Collaboration requires more time, energy, diplomacy, and patience than deciding alone, though, so product owners can't afford to make every decision through collaboration—it should be reserved only for those decisions that are complex and require a great deal of buy-in.

The final quadrant in the matrix is for decisions that are complex but don't require much buy-in. An example here could be choosing which third-party products to integrate with or which technology to build the product on. In these situations, great product owners tend to adopt a "consult then decide" strategy. These are the decisions that are too risky to delegate, are not contentious enough to require buy-in, yet still require the advice of experts. For decisions like these, great product owners gather as much information and advice as they can and then make a decision.

Create a Matrix of Influence

Most quadrants of the decision-making matrix rely on collaborating with, delegating decisions to, or consulting with stakeholders—not all of whom will be on the product owner team, even if one exists.

Simply put, a stakeholder is anyone who has a stake in the product, who is affected by it, or who shows an interest in it. More specifically, stakeholders are those whose help is needed to develop, release, and provide the product. Exactly what role these stakeholders hold will be specific to each product and company.

Identifying stakeholders, however, is only half the battle. With so many people competing for their time and attention, product owners need to be able to understand the optimal way to engage with each type of stakeholder. The following matrix, adopted from *"Strategic Management of Stakeholders: Theory and Practice,"* published by Ackerman and Eden in 2011, can help product owners better focus their efforts, quickly generate the desired buy-in, and spend their time more wisely.

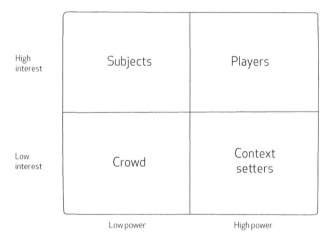

Figure D-3. Creating a Matrix of Influence can optimise stakeholder engagement.

Inform the Crowd

The crowd is the easiest group of stakeholders to deal with as these people are firstly not very interested in the product and secondly don't have the power to influence product decisions. Many product owners view the crowd as *potential* stakeholders; the crowd aren't interested or influential enough at the moment to have much of a say in the final product.

It is usually sufficient to simply keep the crowd informed. Giving them access to the product's wiki web page or sending out a status report to update them on important developments is typically good enough.

Consult the Context Setters

As the name suggests, the context setters affect the product's context but they take little interest in the product itself. In some circumstances context setters impact the product only because they wield a large amount of power. For example, regulatory bodies or the media (neither of whom has a direct interest in getting involved in the development of the product) may still have the power to affect its success. Because they are typically involved in critiquing or enforcing rules for the released product, context setters are alternatively known as referees.

Great product owners ensure that the context setters feel that their opinions, concerns, and ideas are heard and understood or at least ensure that the development of the product doesn't upset the context setters. This is usually achieved by regularly consulting the context setters through one-on-one meetings.

Great product owners don't allow the context setters to dictate decisions or intimidate them. Instead, great product owners are tactful yet strong and have the courage to say no when appropriate, even when faced with a powerful, or even pushy, context setter.

Involve the Subjects

The third group of stakeholders are the subjects. Subjects have a keen interest in the project and may well be very affected by decisions, yet they have very little influence or power. Instead they are *subject* to the product owner's decisions, hence the name.

Great product owners do not take advantage of this group's lack of influence. On the contrary, great product owners actively engage subjects on a regular basis. For instance, they might invite subjects to sprint review meetings and encourage them to share their feedback. If managed well, this group of stakeholders can be turned into strong allies and advocates for the product. That doesn't mean, however, that product owners should agree to every idea or request the subjects raise.

Many product owners consider their consumers and users to be members of the subjects category; and for those organisations that develop their products with little to no transparency or opportunity for feedback from their user bases, this might be an accurate categorisation. However, product owners for agile organisations recognise that even if consumers and users fall into the subjects category during development, they have a tremendous impact on the success of the final product. Therefore, great product owners purposefully seek feedback from their consumers and users early and often during development, ensuring that their influence is felt during product direction rather than after the product's release.

Collaborate with the Players

The players are the most important partners for any product owner, and they should collaborate closely with them in the product development effort. Players not only have a strong interest in product decisions but they also hold a very strong influence over product direction. They are likely to be directly affected by any decisions and will be very keen to know what is going on at all times.

Great product owners aim to secure the buy-in of the players, establishing close and trusting relationships with them. They attempt to listen to the players' feedback and, wherever possible, incorporate their ideas and knowledge. Players want to be involved with the product on a continuous basis; good product owners understand the benefit of this close collaboration to the development of the product.

Because of the sheer number of stakeholders in this quadrant and because of their importance, great product owners invest most of their time and energy in managing the players. Collaboration itself is not easy and requires both humility and assertiveness. Great product owners, for example, aim to build consensus with the players but never shy away from difficult conversations. They don't settle for the smallest common denominator and have the courage to make a decision if no agreement can be achieved. I'll talk more specifically about collaboration in "Negotiable" later in this book.

Decide to Trust Yourself and Others

Throughout this chapter, I've made the case that product owners need to be decisive. That includes being courageous enough to make decisions precisely when they need to be made and refusing to dodge difficult decisions. Being decisive isn't just about making decisions, though; it's also about knowing when not to make decisions. Great product owners are wise enough to know when delaying a decision is the right thing to do, yet they also understand that delivering quickly is the best way to reduce the cost of a bad decisions. The best product owners know how to balance these two competing needs. Product development is a complex, ongoing activity. Therefore, great product owners create and maintain a decision-making strategy. They know they cannot possess all the knowledge to make every decision, and so they seek advice and counsel from domain experts or even a product owner team. They actively increase engagement and generate buy-in by involving the right people in the decision-making process.

The life of a great product owner is a busy one. A sensible and sustainable decision-making process allows product owners to focus their limited time in the most important areas, which not only helps make a demanding role a bit easier, but also makes product owners much more effective in the long term.

What worries you about trusting yourself or others?

How realistic and based in objective fact are these concerns?

DRIVEN

Ruthless

"A vain man can never be utterly ruthless: he wants to win applause and therefore he accommodates himself to others"
Johan Wolfgang von Goethe

As I alluded to in the previous chapter, at times product owners need to be ruthless in their decision making. Please don't misunderstand ruthless in this context to mean brutal, cruel, or unwilling to collaborate or compromise. Instead, ruthless refers to the idea that product owners cannot allow sentiment to undermine what is best for the product, the organisation, the users and the customers. As such, great product owners understand the need to mercilessly reject certain features and even products, at least for now, in favour of those that are more valuable.

Value is not a simple one-dimensional factor. The value a product delivers to the organisation might be revenue generation or it might be customer acquisition or it might be technological consolidation. Sometimes the most valuable endeavor might be to expose risk—to find flaws and problems early so that either the team has time to address them or product development can be stopped before too much money has been invested. Sometimes value is a combination of all of these factors. Regardless, great product owners are ruthless in their efforts to clarify what value is and then deliver it.

As we will see in the upcoming stories, great product owners are those who take a firm stand on the priority needs of the product, even in the face of disagreements and obstacles, to ensure the most valuable features and products are realised first.

"I feel strongly that the plan I've laid out will work.
But that doesn't mean executing it is going to be easy."

Rank and File

Good product owners know what is needed.
Great product owners know what can wait.

"Let's have a coffee break, everyone. We've done really well and I think we deserve some fresh air and caffeine," Tom said.

Tom sat back in his chair for the first time in two hours. As the product owner for an important new product launch, he had been working tirelessly with his stakeholders to visualise the best possible product for their customers. He was always amazed at how many ideas grew out of a group effort like this—there was no way he would have thought of most of these features on his own. Even so, as he sat looking at a whiteboard filled to overflowing from a remarkably creative and productive collaboration session, he began to worry about the next portion of the meeting. The brutal reality was that somehow they had to trim that brilliant list of features, ideas and wishes down to only the most important set of features—those that would enable them to release the first version of the product as quickly as possible.

Tom could still vividly remember some of the nightmare prioritisation sessions at his previous company. They had used a three-level priority system:

Priority 1 (P1): The most important requirements

Priority 2 (P2): Still important but not as important as P1 requirements

Priority 3 (P3): Less important still than P2 requirements.

On the face of it, this common-sense grouping had seemed reasonable. Soon, however, Tom had realised that almost everything on the product backlog he had inherited seemed to be a P1! Because of this Tom had no idea as to which P1 requirement truly was the most important or how to choose from amongst the competing requirements.

When he had expressed his concern to another product owner who had been with the company longer, that product owner had told Tom he'd created a new category called Priority Zero (P0) to describe the most important P1 requirements. Tom chuckled to himself as, thinking about it now, he wouldn't be surprised if that company now used a Priority Minus One (P-1) for the truly, truly important P1 requirements!

When the other stakeholders returned from their coffee break, Tom decided to share that prioritisation story with them. The stakeholders laughed at the ridiculousness of the category escalation.

"Surely they knew that not everything could be a P1?" someone asked.

"On some level, they did," Tom replied. "But they also recognised that, with so many competing concerns, if a requirement wasn't considered a P1, it might not ever be implemented. So eventually everyone began making business cases for why their requirements were indeed P1."

Tom paused for a moment to let that sink in then continued. "The reality is, though, that if everything is high priority, nothing is high priority. This kind of priority inflation makes it extremely difficult to do what's best for the product."

The stakeholders were silent for a moment as they looked at the full whiteboard of fabulous ideas—they could immediately see how tempting it would be to ask for them all.

Jon, the VP of Marketing, spoke up. "We laugh at Tom's previous company, but I've got to say, I'm not sure how we're going to take this huge list and narrow it down. I love all of these ideas, especially my own!" he quipped. Everyone chuckled again. "But in all seriousness, Tom, how do you suggest we proceed?"

"Product owners have to be ruthless in establishing priorities. And to do that, I have to know what is truly most valuable—and something always is. One way I got that across at my last company was to call them out on their priority inflation. I explained that if everything truly is important, then it shouldn't matter which one is done first. I then suggested that we allow the development team to pick the next feature to implement."

"So you just let the team pick?" Jon asked incredulously. "What happened?"

"It was very interesting," Tom said. "The first thing I noticed was that the team, which had been weighed down by the continuous stream of high-priority items, regained some enthusiasm. The second thing I noticed was that the stakeholders and I recoiled at some of the choices. We looked at each other as if to say, 'Whoah! Not *that* one!' So if nothing else, we instantly knew that at least some of the items weren't *quite* the highest priority."

There were more chuckles from the stakeholders.

Tom continued, "Using the team-pick approach served two purposes: It demonstrated that there really were some features that were more important than others and it empowered the team. But we knew that if we wanted to create the right product, we needed to come up with a prioritisation system that worked. We all agreed that although the P1, P2 and P3 buckets made it easy—too easy—for people to group things; it wasn't granular enough. It didn't show how much *more* valuable P1 was than P2. So we decided to try stack ranking. Basically, what that meant was that no two items could have the same priority. Instead, each item is assigned a value that is expressed in relationship to the value of the other items. We used a measure I called Tom Dollars, so some items were worth 500 Tom Dollars, others only 50. To help people assign a realistic value, we defined certain value factors relative to the product vision."

After a bit of discussion around value factors and vision, the stakeholders agreed to try a stacked ranking process.

Tom said, "Here's what I propose, then. For the first release, I want to target a few key customers who are dissatisfied with their current provider." He went on to provide more details about the first customer group.

Then Tom explained his plan to evolve the vision over time: "I believe that if we get that customer segment on board first, we will not only get some revenue but we will also make a bit of a splash. Then, in release 2, we can expand and add the extra features that will allow us to increase the user base. Finally, in release 3, we can focus on the high-margin areas.

As he looked around the room, Tom could see by the nods and thoughtful expressions that everyone seemed to understand the logic of his approach. He decided to take this moment to appeal to the stakeholders for their assistance in making the vision a reality:

"I feel strongly that the plan I've laid out will work. But that doesn't mean executing it is going to be easy," he said, gesturing to the full whiteboard. "All of these features are important and valuable, but the reality is that we probably can't afford to do everything and we certainly can't afford to do everything at once. So I will need your help to be ruthless with this list. If we can't agree, I'll make the final call, but everything will go much more smoothly if we all are on the same page about how we are prioritising the features."

The rest of the workshop went well. When disagreements arose, Tom steered everyone back to the vision and the relative value weighting. On the occasions where the stakeholders couldn't reach consensus, Tom made the decision himself and kept the meeting moving forward. After two hours, the group had agreed on the first release for the product: A Minimal Viable Product (MVP) that consisted of only the most valuable features for their initial customer group.

What is the absolute minimum that the product would need to do for it to be releasable?

Remember No Means Not Now

In this story, Tom and his stakeholders worked together to create a long wish list of features. The problem was that, although in theory everyone agreed the product couldn't include everything—at least not all at once—in practice, it can be difficult to say no.

Several factors make ruthless prioritisation difficult, especially for people who are new to the product owner role. The first is a tendency to want to keep everyone happy—to give in and try to give all the stakeholders at least some of the features they have requested. As the old adage from Aesop's Fables goes: "Please all, and you will please none." Nowhere is that more true than in developing a product.

Stakeholders, users, customers—even the development team—all have competing needs and compelling reasons why their proposed solutions should be the highest priority. When product owners try to take all of these needs into account at one time, they end up with a bloated backlog of must-do features and no way to decide which to do first. The resulting product, if the team can cobble one together, is likely to be a mixed-up mess rather than a targeted, purposeful release.

The second factor that interferes with effective prioritisation is that it is difficult to cope with loss, even if it's only the loss of an idea.

Once you have invested in something, even only to the point of imagining and writing a user story, you don't want to see that effort wasted by cutting it. People can experience tangible grief over letting go—whether it's letting go of a focus on a particular customer segment or of a favourite feature, even if it is only for right now. They fear, and sometimes rightfully so, that if they don't push for their ideas, they will never be implemented. As a result, the product backlog grows and grows, while the product flounders.

The key to overcoming both of these natural tendencies is to do what Tom did in the story and what Stephen Covey recommends in his *Seven Habits of Highly Effective People* : Have a bigger "yes!" burning inside (149). In other words, focus everyone on a well-defined vision—the big, burning yes—and objectively evaluate each feature based on whether it is essential for fulfilling that vision or not. Then remind everyone that though you are saying "No, not now" to some requests, you are not saying, "Not ever." Alleviate their concerns by showing them a plan for how the vision will evolve to include more of the lower priority features.

Ruthless prioritisation is both that simple and that difficult. Let's look next at some practical things you can do to make it easier.

Do you have a roadmap for the product over the next 6-18 months?

Are other people aware of this?

Stack Rank the Backlog

In the story, Tom relays his experiences with prioritisation groups and why he prefers a more ruthless stack ranking system. Let's review the key points he made.

Firstly, prioritisation groups take many forms:

- P1, P2, P3
- High, Medium, Low
- MoSCoW – Must, Should, Could, Won't
- Mandatory, Critical and Urgent!

Yet, while these might seem like good ways to organise competing features, the end result is that they quickly become too coarse-grained to be helpful, especially the high-priority features. When multiple features all carry the same priority (e.g., P1 or P0), it's impossible to know which features are truly the most valuable.

In the story, Tom shares an experience where he inherited a huge bucket of P1 features and a group of stakeholders who insisted that no features in that bucket were more important than others. To alleviate the gridlock and to drive home the point that some features are, in fact, more valuable than others, Tom allowed the development team to fill an iteration with any set of features they wanted from the P1 bucket. Although the team delighted in finally making some progress, the stakeholders had a much more visceral reaction to the team's choices. This proved Tom's point: Some features were clearly more important than others, so the stakeholders needed a better way to distinguish the most valuable features.

Stack ranking clearly delineates among many high-priority features by enforcing the rule that no two items can have the same priority. Rank is determined by an item's relative valuation – in other words its value relative to the other items.

#	Feature	Value
1	---	$1000
2	---	$900
3	---	$850
4	---	$849
5	---	$800
6	---	$799
7	---	$750
8	---	$500
9	---	$475
10	---	$450
11	---	$430
12	---	$300
13	---	$250

Figure R-1. Stack ranking helps to distinguish amongst high priority features.

In the story, Tom used Tom Dollars as the unit of measure for value, but any unit that makes sense in your context will work. The general idea is as follows: No item can have the same value as another and each feature's value should be calculated in relation to the other features. As an example, in Figure R-1, Item 10 has a value of 450

Tom Dollars. Item 2, however, is twice as valuable, so it has a value of 900 Tom Dollars.

What do you think your users would be willing to pay for the various items on your product backlog?

Like any rule, "no two items can have the same priority" can be taken too far. It's arguably not necessary to distinguish between a priority 1 and a priority 2 item: Both will likely get done in the first iteration. However, knowing which item is priority 9 and which item is priority 10 could mean the difference between which item gets delivered in the first iteration and which one has to be delayed until the second iteration.

At the lower end of the priority scale, extreme granularity begins to add less value again. For example, worrying about whether something is priority 199 or priority 200 isn't worth it, especially if the team typically delivers 8-10 items per iteration. At that pace of delivery, it's not very likely that the team will actually get to work on those items anyway.

Most great product owners tend to take a pragmatic approach to prioritisation. They are ruthless about prioritisation granularity at the top end of the backlog, but take advantage of prioritisation groups towards the lower end of their product backlog.

Follow the Vision

To once again quote Stephen Covey, "You have to decide what your highest priorities are and have the courage—pleasantly, smilingly, nonapologetically—to say 'no' to other things. ... The enemy of the 'best' is often the 'good'" (157). People have a natural tendency to want to say yes to everything and to hold on to every good idea. Yet good product owners know that in order to create the best product, they must say no (or at least not now) even to ideas they like and learn to let go.

That's why great product owners tend to share a similar pattern for prioritisation. They communicate a vision, allow for evolution, determine value factors, and decide on a finite list of features for the next (or initial) version of the product. That pattern is shown and described in more detail in Figure R-2.

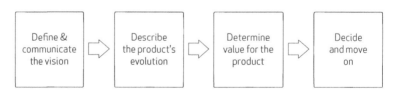

Figure R-2. Great product owners share a similar pattern for prioritisation.

Great product owners invest their energy in **defining and communicating a cohesive, value-focused vision** for the product so each feature's contribution towards that vision can be assessed. Developing a common understanding amongst stakeholders has the secondary benefit of allowing the wider group to collaborate on making the decisions, reducing the pressure on the product owner. To develop an effective vision great product owners identify the specific niche and/or the specific demographic to be targeted. While they might be tempted to create a super-product that satisfies everyone, they understand that most successful products are narrow in scope and targeted to a specific audience.

Next, great product owners reassure their stakeholders by **describing the product's evolution.** They remind everyone that value can be delivered – and risk reduced – early when using an iterative process. They know that focusing on the bare minimum functionality - or Minimal Viable Product - will enable the organisation to get the product to market (or at least get empirical feedback) quickly. They are willing to say "not now" to certain features in order to strip out the "important but not critical" features.

To help make stack ranking possible, great product owners also **determine what value means** for their defined vision. Most products have many value factors, from customer retention to customer acquisition; from market differentiation to integrating product lines; from embracing new technologies to becoming more competitive. Great product owners pull together all of the various facets of value and communicate their importance so that everyone is aware of what this particular product development effort is hoping to achieve. Well-defined value factors help the wider team determine the relative value of the features within the product backlog without the need for detailed micro-management.

> What factors do you consider when prioritising the product backlog?
>
> Value? Cost? Risk? Learning? Uncertainty? Novelty? Dependencies?

The first three factors in the pattern shown in Figure R-2 are all aimed at engaging the stakeholders in the process of determining which features will and will not be in the initial product release. By defining the vision, evolution, and value factors, great product owners involve others in the decision-making and product development process. Sometimes, however, great product owners have to put data, analysis, and negotiation to one side and, for the good of the product, just **decide and move on**. The best product owners realise that this trump card is always there for them, but they play it only when it's really necessary.

Reset When You Struggle

Letting go of an idea is difficult for most people; product owners are no exception. If you struggle with being ruthless, don't judge yourself harshly. Instead, acknowledge what is happening and reset.

Great product owners train themselves to become aware of when they are becoming too emotionally attached to an idea and losing touch with reason. They also develop personal strategies to help return to a more ruthless frame of mind so that they are able once again to make an objective evaluation.

These strategies typically involve the following:

- Buy time and find some space to clear the mind.
- Focus on the positive side of the decision. Remember that by being ruthless you are giving something a greater chance of success. Focus on that aspect more than what you are potentially letting go of.
- Talk things through with a completely neutral party – perhaps a coach, a friend, a spouse or a child. This neutral party is often a great mirror to help highlight assumptions and hidden biases.
- Evaluate the cost as well as the value of doing something. These costs include opportunity costs (by doing one thing we cannot do something else) and the ongoing costs (support costs, maintenance costs, complexity costs for example).

Being ruthless requires courage; there is no sugar-coating that fact. Great product owners know that making ruthless choices among competing interests is a part of their job. To help make it easier, they remember that every no is actually a not now on an evolving agile project. They also employ stack ranking to help distinguish amongst competing high-priority features. Great product owners evaluate every feature's value against a backdrop of clear product vision, and share that vision and their decisions with the stakeholders. Then, when the circumstances call for it, they are willing to ruthlessly make a choice and move forward, knowing that in doing so they are giving their product the greatest chance of success.

"I have to be honest, though, and admit it isn't what we had hoped for"

Hold and Fold

Good product owners take calculated gambles.
Great product owners also know when to walk away.

The previous chapter's story ended when Tom and his stakeholders identified the necessary features for the first release. His work didn't end there, though. His next challenge, was to work out how long it would take to deliver that release.

To help make that happen, Sal, the ScrumMaster, booked a great venue for an offsite release planning workshop. It not only had enough space for everyone to collaborate, it also had some extra areas for breaking out into small groups. Because most of the stakeholders and the development team had arrived the night before for a meal and to get to know each other a bit, the mood seemed really positive as Sal and Tom stood together to kick the day off.

Sal explained the agenda and objectives for the day and quickly handed over to Tom, who set the scene by explaining the product vision. Tom then went on to briefly explain the process he went through with the stakeholders to define the various facets of value and ruthlessly hone in on the MVP for release 1.

The team were surprised by the content of the release, as many of the features the stakeholders had made a lot of noise about in the past hadn't made the cut. At the same time, the team members held a largely unspoken appreciation for the difficult but valuable process Tom had gone through.

Tom then turned things over to the team, saying: "This list of features is the bare minimum number of features that we need in order to have a viable first release. What I need from you are estimates for each of the features. The goal of this estimation is to determine if the release is possible given our time constraints and to give me the information I need to refine the prioritisation, taking risk and cost into account."

With Sal acting as facilitator, the team determined their capacity for the coming sprints, chose an appropriate sprint length, and began to estimate the work. They broke out into multiple groups to estimate, while Tom rotated among the different groups, answering questions and providing greater detail so that the team could give estimates with a greater confidence level.

At the end of the estimation timebox, the team reconvened. Sal turned to Tom and said, "We estimate that it'll take six months to get the MVP done. And by *done*, we mean actually ready for the users to start using."

Tom and the rest of the stakeholders were visibly disappointed. Tom said, "OK. Thank you for all of the work you did to arrive at that estimate. I have to be honest, though, and admit it isn't what we had hoped for. We need to release in five months in order to beat one of our competitors to market. And we had only budgeted about

£250,000 to develop the MVP—and this would cost £300,000. I'm not sure what to do right now about a six-month timeline."

Tom paused for a moment, then continued. "We're all due for a coffee break anyway. Sal, would you and the development team mind giving me and the stakeholders about 30 minutes to talk privately about everything we've learned today? We need to talk about the product, revisit our priorities, and consider all of our options before moving forward."

"Sure," said Sal. "We could use a break, anyway. See you all in thirty minutes."

As the development team left the room, Tom spoke to the stakeholders, "Let's take five minutes to get ourselves some coffee and then meet up in the break-out room for a quick chat."

After they had all made their way to the break out room, Tom immediately named the elephant in the room.

"Six months is disappointing. I know we were all hoping for five months for lots of reasons. I was tempted to start negotiating with the development team immediately, but I decided it might be better to step back and chat this through together before we respond."

As Tom expected, Rico, the marketing manager, stressed how important it was to get out ahead of the competition: "If we are beaten to market, we will be playing catch up forever. Surely, we can negotiate with the team on this. They have probably built some slack into their estimates."

"Maybe, said Tom. "But I've worked with this team before. If they say it will take six months, it will take at least that long—possibly even a bit longer depending on what they learn when they start creating something real."

Rico shook his head vehemently. "That will never work. We need it sooner."

Tom nodded. "I know. And we've cut the functionality down to the bare minimum, so I don't see any way to remove any features in order to release the product sooner."

Tom paused and looked around the room. Everyone nodded in agreement.

"What about overtime? Or bringing on more team members?" asked Rico.

"Well, first, remember that we are working with a finite budget, so we can't add more manpower—and even if we did it doesn't often speed things up, at least not right away. Ironically enough, at first it tends to actually slow things down. Second, asking the team to work beyond its capacity will likely result in a load of technical debt. I think we'd regret it in the long run."

"What do you mean by technical debt?" asked Rico.

Tom got up and drew a diagram on the flipchart sheet at the front of the room. The diagram showed the same amount of work being delivered in a shorter time frame. He shaded in the area between the two lines and turned back towards the stakeholders.

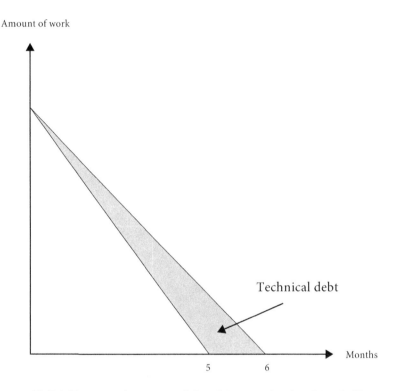

Fig R-3. *Trying to achieve 6 months' work in 5 months of work inevitably leads to technical debt*

"If we "encourage" the team to agree to five months instead of six, the team would probably agree to do it, "Tom said. "But they won't just wake up a bit cleverer. And the work won't magically become easier. So to get it done, they will inevitably cut a few corners—and they might also squeeze the amount of time available for testing just a bit. Plus, they will likely have to work a few long days and the odd weekend, getting tired and sloppy as a result. In the end, they might meet the deadline, but the final result will be a lower quality product (sometimes on purpose and sometimes out of sheer exhaustion). In other words, we've introduced technical debt—and we'll end up repaying that debt (with interest) later."

"But we could go back and fix the quality issues once we have released, right?" asked Rico.

"Maybe. But there are a couple of problems. Firstly, there is usually a lag time between cutting quality and seeing the consequences, so we might not be able to spot it straight away. And if we can't see it, we can't fix it," replied Tom.

"Secondly, working beyond team capacity sets unrealistic expectations about our speed while simultaneously slowing us down."

"How does it slow us down?" asked Rico.

"Two ways. Firstly, by creating a lower quality product we increase our maintenance costs. It's going to be harder to add new functionality to the product because things don't work as expected," Tom explained. "And then, on top of that, the team will be overworked, so they will have lower energy and less morale."

Amount of work

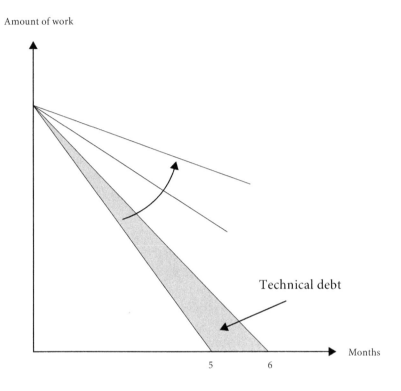

Technical debt

Months

5   6

Fig R-4. As technical debt rises, the team's velocity falls.

"Fair enough, Tom, I see your point—it's a slippery slope," said Rico. "So what do we do?"

"The only thing we can realistically do is to assume that the development team's estimates are correct and ask ourselves one simple question."

Tom wrote on the flipchart:

Given it is likely to take six months, are we justified in starting this project?

Rico was appalled. "Not do it at all? Just based on this team's say-so? I'm not willing to let go of all the work and all the planning we've done so far. This product could be a difference maker!"

"But only if it's out in 5 months, comes in on budget, and actually delights our customers once it's out there," Tom countered. "Listen, I'm not keen to let go of this idea either. One thing we have in our favour is that we don't necessarily have to decide on the whole project right now. By working in iterations we should have some tangible data about the likely outcome every iteration.

"So here's what I suggest. Let's commit to one or two sprint's worth of work. If, at the end of that time, the team's estimates remain unchanged or we cannot find any functionality to cut, we stop the project completely. We're investing a little to avoid wasting a lot."

Everyone agreed to fund the project one sprint at a time and then reassess. After two sprints, however, it was clear that the team would not be able to deliver the MVP in five months—and despite many efforts to find features to cut, the stakeholders couldn't reduce the size of the MVP. Tom made the hard choice to cancel the project.

Fold a Losing Hand

That was a brutal story. Tom did all of the right things in guiding the stakeholder team through the development of an MVP and in accepting the reality of the situation. The team did all the right things by coming forward with a realistic estimate. And the stakeholders did the right things too—sacrificing time, money, and their own pet features for the good of the overall project. And still, the project had to be canceled. A loss like that can be crushing.

It can be so crushing, in fact, that many organisations would choose to just keep going, either pushing the team to deliver early with lower quality or releasing after the desired date and hoping for the best—to escalate their commitment and give in to the *sunk cost fallacy*, which is discussed more fully later in this chapter. In contrast, Tom displays many attributes of a great product owner by having the courage to ruthlessly reject this project when it's clear it won't achieve its goals.

First, Tom displayed a remarkable degree of mindfulness. When the team came back with an estimate that didn't fit his needs, Tom expressed his disappointment in a calm and measured way. He focused on the facts and purposefully avoided placing any blame. He then asked for a bit of a time out so that he and the stakeholders could reflect and reassess.

 What can you do to ensure that your reactions to information are more calm and measured?

Tom also demonstrated significant restraint. Remember that he and the stakeholders had just been through the wrenching exercise of trimming an enormous list of exciting features into a small, targeted release. Now, he was faced with the possibility that even this heavily pruned feature set would not fit within their desired timebox and budget. Rather than push back emotionally, Tom was able to step back and view the problem objectively. He framed the situation in matter-of-fact terms and had well-reasoned arguments against stop-gap solutions such as overtime, adding manpower, or accepting a sub-par project and fixing it later.

Throughout the story, Tom models excellent coping skills when dealing with loss. He lessens the blow of letting go of desired features by saying "not now", instead of "never". Then, he absorbs the loss of a plan he and his stakeholders had felt certain would be possible. He does this first by admitting that the plan was only that—a plan—and that any certainty surrounding that, or any, plan was false to begin with. Tom further eases the pain by reducing the commitment to the project to just fund one sprint at a time and then reassess. He then uses data and empirical evidence to ultimately make the decision to let go of the project entirely.

Assume you are going to make some mistakes. How could you make those mistakes cheaper, faster and easier to recover from?

Not every product owner or team accepts ambiguity so gracefully. Instead, people tend to focus on the "best case" or "worst case" scenario when actually it's probably going to be neither. That's why it's so vital not to make decisions in a vacuum but instead to hear from multiple perspectives when trying to determine the best course of action. Great product owners surround themselves with teams that are cross-functional and that represent multiple levels of experience.

In the story, Tom is able to be ruthless at least in part because his decisions are supported by technically sound agile practices, including release planning and iterative development. The next sections look more closely at how these valuable practices aid ruthless prioritisation and decision making, even to the point of walking away entirely.

Learn from Release Planning

Release planning is a term used by Scrum teams to explain the process they go through when attempting to answer one of two questions:

1. How much functionality can we build by this date? or
2. How long will it take to build this set of functionality?

Great product owners operate on the principle that "all plans are imprecise and will be proven wrong." They also know that the further out into the future a team is planning, the greater the degree of inaccuracy. But even though a plan is destined to be wrong, it can still be useful. And often, merely the act of planning as a collaborative team, and the learning that happens in that space, is more valuable than the actual artefact of the plan.

While the release planning process doesn't follow a strict format, it typically includes a number of common elements, as shown in the figure below.

Figure R-5. Release planning sessions typically include these elements.

In the story, we first saw Sal book an appropriate space for the meeting. Then, Tom shared the vision, product backlog, and rationale for his initial prioritisation. With that information in mind, Sal and the team determined their capacity, chose an appropriate sprint length for the project, and estimated the items that Tom and the stakeholders had chosen as the MVP for the first release. During this process, they also defined what *done* would mean for the project.

Estimation is a complex and inherently inaccurate process that is beyond the scope of this book, primarily because it is not a product owner responsibility. However, it is important to understand that one of the principles of agile methods such as Scrum is that the people doing the work should do the estimating. Some product owners are nervous and suspicious of team's estimations—I have witnessed many a game of bluff and double bluff, inflation and negotiation, being played. That being said, on the whole, product owners who genuinely trust their teams to estimate and who do what they can to reduce the potential negative consequences of "wrong estimates" get by far the best results.

Do you know what motivates your team to take greater ownership, responsibility and pride of their work?

Once the team's estimate is in, the product owner is left with a decision as to whether to move forward or to cancel the project. The next section looks more closely at how agile processes help make this decision a bit easier.

Decide, Build, Decide Again

In the story, Tom asks a question every product owner should pose after release planning: *Given what we know right now, are we justified in starting this project?* Every product owner needs to make a judgment call on whether to take a gamble on the first sprint.

Prior to beginning a project, good product owners take the information they have gleaned from market research and release planning to determine whether to proceed with the idea or not. In Tom's case, he decides that it is worth the gamble to give sprint one the green light. In other words, he delays a decision on the project as a whole until he collects some actual data.

The team builds one sprint's worth of features and then Tom has the opportunity to decide again: Are we justified in continuing this project? This isn't just a question for projects that are considered a gamble. Every product owner should ask this question after every sprint, even if the initial plans suggested that the project is a "sure thing." Great product owners know there is simply no such thing— every project has a degree of uncertainty built in.

After two sprints, Tom and the stakeholders stop the project. Rather than waste the rest of their budget, they cut their losses and move on to something else. It's a difficult decision—and a ruthless one—but it is sometimes the right decision to make.

Avoid Escalation of Commitment

Anyone who has played poker knows the term "pot committed," the realisation that even if you are holding a losing hand you cannot fold because you have bet so much money already. Economists call this the sunk cost fallacy, a tendency to justify spending more and more money or time on a bad investment based on the amount that has already been spent. Other common terms to describe this phenomenon are "in for a penny, in for a pound" and "throwing good money after bad."

This escalation of commitment is irrational but oh, so human! The reality is the money or time you've already invested is sunk no matter what you decide now; you can't get it back. So great product owners ruthlessly choose their course of action based only on where the project currently stands and the probable outcome of their next decision.

Consider Other Options

So far, I've only talked about the need for product owners to let go of features or even sometimes entire projects. Part of being a DRIVEN product owner, however, is being ruthless enough to choose a different team for a project or to root out impediments that are preventing a team from reaching their goals.

Sometimes the project is achievable but the chosen delivery team is not capable of delivering high enough quality at a fast enough pace. In these situations, the product owner has a tough decision to make. They have the opportunity to replace the team (or perhaps certain members of the team) with one that is more capable or, if they are taking more of a long-term view, they may choose to support the development of the team and facilitate their upskilling through training or experience.

Other times, the problem is that too many impediments are preventing the team from doing what needs to be done. In this situation, the team would look to the ScrumMaster to provide greater support and facilitation such that they can be as effective as possible. Great product owners tend to see the removal of impediments as opportunities to help the team deliver better and quicker and so decide to join in the effort of impediment removal themselves rather than simply leave it to a ScrumMaster. Ruthlessly tracking down and eradicating the causes of team dysfunction and frustration could be another part of a product owner's job.

Product owners are accountable for deciding yes or no on a project but team members and ScrumMasters are accountable for their own performance as well. This is rarely spoken about in agile circles and may seem harsh, but the lifecycle of a product development effort is often so tight that ruthless changes are often required. The best product owners tend to take a long-term, developmental approach to relationships within the development organisation but know how to make the tough decisions when they are warranted.

DRIVEN

Informed

"Real knowledge is to know the extent of one's ignorance."
Confucius

The most common complaint from agile development teams is lack of product owner availability. It's so common, in fact, that I almost included *available* as one of the characteristics.

However, I suspect that many agile teams' complaints are not simply about a lack of availability but just as much to do with how productive the limited time is that product owners have. Many product owners tend to be stretched so thin that they are distracted, unprepared, or just "not there" even when they are technically in the room or reachable via phone or email. After all, I could be available 100 percent of the time but if I am ill equipped or don't have the head space to make decisions then what use will I be?

That brings us to the paradox of knowledge and the product owner. Good product owners are informed: they research their product space, the market they are launching it in, and the potential purchasers, consumers, and users of their product. With this information they position the product and the development effort for the greatest chance of success.

However, as discussed in "Decisive," DRIVEN product owners also understand that they cannot realistically gain all the knowledge they'd like before making every decision. They know that some decisions will have to be made using incomplete information. So great product owners couple research and knowledge with the opportunities to learn that an agile process offers them.

The next two stories illustrate the two sides to this particular coin.

"No, no, no…you've completely missed the point there."

Trust and Verify

Good product owners trust their instincts.
Great product owners find data to test their ideas.

Until recently, product owner Mike had been feeling a bit smug about the job he had been doing and how well product development was going. The first five review meetings had gone off without a hitch. The team had delivered what they had promised and the stakeholders had remarked how happy they were with the progress being made. They had also praised Mike specifically for his ability to take their requirements and turn them into something that met their needs. Mike had been really pleased with that feedback because most of the time he had needed to decipher, re-imagine, or even take his best guess at some of the feature requests, either because what the stakeholder was asking for was really vague, was not possible, or simply conflicted with what another key stakeholder wanted.

However, over the last few sprints, Mike's intuition seemed to have deserted him. The feedback in the last sprint review in particular had left him and the team incredibly frustrated.

"That's no good," one stakeholder said about a feature.

"No, no, no...you've completely missed the point there," said somebody else about another.

"The way you've built that will actually create more work for us, not make things easier," said a third stakeholder.

Outwardly, Mike had said all of the right things. He had thanked the stakeholders for their feedback, stated how the sprint review is specifically designed to enable important learning such as this, and had reinforced how great it was that they found this out now rather than later. Inwardly, however, he was disappointed. By looking around the room, he could tell the development team were just as crestfallen as he was.

Mike had decided there and then that he would go and see some of the users in action – it had been a while since he had taken a trip up north to the office where the majority of the stakeholders were located. And he was determined to take one of the developers with him. Stef was the first to volunteer.

On the journey, Mike took the opportunity to get to know Stef a little better. They spent a good part of the journey discussing their shared interest in fishing, telling stories and discussing favourite locations and baits to use. Eventually, the conversation turned to work and the frustration they both had felt after the most recent feedback from the stakeholders.

"I feel a bit guilty because I know that you put a lot of effort into those features," Mike said.

"Well to be honest I am feeling a bit frustrated because I'm probably going to have to do those features all over again. I can't help think about the wasted time. I hate waste," Stef admitted.

"I know exactly what you mean," said Mike, nodding his head in agreement. "Although I genuinely believe it's not going to turn out to be a total waste. I've learned my lesson about making assumptions and am determined that it won't happen again. That's one of the reasons we're on this trip. I've booked a meeting room and arranged some time with Linda and some of her team to go through a few of the upcoming requirements. The next set of requirements are all focused on replacing a manual process that they have been using for years so I'm hoping that we can clarify a few things from their perspective by talking things through with them."

Stef was quiet for a moment, and then said, "I was wondering if we might take the opportunity to do a little more than talking."

"How so?" asked Mike.

"Well sometimes when the team is planning out how we are going to build some new features, we do a bit of low-fi prototyping, where we simulate what the product could do in a semi-tangible way," explained Stef.

"I like the sound of that," Mike said. "Tell me more."

Together, Mike and Stef plotted a new course of action for their meeting, which they decided to reframe as a workshop. During the workshop, Mike asked Linda to walk him through four features, one at a time, demonstrating their current process for dealing with it, what frustrated them with how things currently were, and what they would like to be able to do instead.

While Linda was talking, Stef created basic paper prototypes based on her answers, and then invited Linda and her team to "play" with them. As they worked with the prototypes, Linda and her team explained both how they would use the prototypes and also how they would improve them. They even made changes to the prototypes in real time to reflect their feedback. At the end of the workshop, Linda and her team remarked on how much easier it was to explain a process when they could hold something in their hands, move it around, and even draw on it.

After everyone else left, Stef stayed in the meeting room to turn the paper prototypes into something more real. Meanwhile, Mike observed Linda and her team while they worked. At the end of the day, Stef and Mike went out for some dinner and talked about their day.

Stef said, "I'm really excited about today. I think they will like what I have to show them in the morning before we head back home. It's a really simple electronic version of the paper prototype. There's nothing behind it but it shows what the functionality could be once we build it."

"Brilliant, Stef. Thanks for doing that—I completely agree that we're back on the right track. But I do have a bit of bad news to share with you. I learned some things that surprised me when I watched Linda and her team work today. They were using the functionality from earlier sprints completely differently to how we intended them to use it. It was quite painful to watch actually."

"What do you mean?" Stef asked.

"It turns out that I've been making bad assumptions about how they go about their work from the beginning. It's just only recently that they decided to mention it to us during the reviews," Mike paused and swallowed hard before continuing. "Stef, they have built manual workarounds for almost every feature we've developed so far."

"Why would they do that?" Stef asked, aghast.

"I asked Linda the same thing," exclaimed Mike. "She told me that although the new features weren't perfect, they were so much better than what they had before that they decided they could live with them—that there were more important things to focus on."

Stef closed his eyes in anguish. "I can't believe that we have replaced something that is no longer fit for purpose by building something new that is still unfit for purpose!"

"Me neither," said Mike. "I'm going to ask them tomorrow to continue being as honest as they were during the last review during future reviews. I'm also going to commit to make more trips like this in the near future so that we get a better sense for how they work and what they need. Plus, I've put a story on the product backlog for us to revise the unfit features we've already developed—and I'm going to prioritise it high!"

Recognize and Reduce Bias

Earlier in this book, I wrote about how great product owners learn to make decisions with incomplete information—to move forward in an agile way, knowing that even if they get it wrong they only get it wrong for one iteration. Sometimes part of that on-the-fly decision making involves making an educated guess as to what the client actually needs. In the story above, Mike is actually quite adept at interpreting client needs, to a point. What he learns, however, is that the better you understand your users, the more accurately you can guess as to what they mean by a particular feature request. And that sometimes, the only way to truly understand someone else's perspective is to observe them at work.

The only problem is, we all see events, people, and actions through the filter of our own biases. As the essayist and memoirist Anais Nin famously said: "We don't see the world as it is, we see it as we are". In other words, we often look at a problem or solution and see only what we expect to see. That means that even when we are attempting to learn about others, we may be unable to see through the filters we have in place. Great product owners, therefore, also cultivate an awareness of their own blind spots by paying attention to their cognitive biases.

Put simply, cognitive biases are thinking patterns that can affect people's ability to make good judgement calls or to interpret information effectively. Although there are too many of them to list here, I want to point out one common cognitive bias that is particularly harmful to product owners who want to be well informed: confirmation bias.

Confirmation bias is the tendency to search for, interpret, focus on and remember information in a way that confirms one's own preconceptions. Confirmation bias is pernicious. In fact, a *study from the University of Iowa* found that once people make their minds up about something they are unlikely to change their minds—not because they are stubborn but because they only see the evidence that confirms what they believe to be true. This is because people tend to subconsciously seek out information that backs up their beliefs while simultaneously screening out anything contradictory.

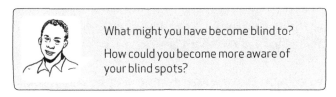

What might you have become blind to?

How could you become more aware of your blind spots?

It is very easy for product owners to be misinformed by data that confirms what they already believe to be true. When this happens, product owners end up defining the product as they think it should be rather than creating the product that consumers and users actually want. This kind of bias appears not only in market-related decisions or predictions but also with regards to impressions of people and relationships. If product owners make up their minds about someone based on initial impressions and don't critically re-assess that opinion then they risk long-term consequences, including the decreased levels of trust and rapport that could prevent them from uncovering better solutions.

Great product owners learn to overcome this natural tendency by purposefully seeking out differing opinions. They might intentionally put someone on their product owner team, for instance, who they know sees the world through a very different lens. Or when conducting a backlog grooming meeting or a sprint review, they might ask for someone to play devil's advocate—to point out the flaws in a proposed solution or the drawbacks of the finished product. Seeing the world through another's eyes can be particularly enlightening. Whether it is observing the user experience first hand or seeking out candid feedback on both the product and the process, great product owners become well informed by learning how to recognize and compensate for their own blind spots.

> Who might be able to increase your ability to see things from a more neutral, objective perspective?

Do the Research

Henry Ford is often credited with saying, "If I had asked people what they wanted, they would have said faster horses." This is used as evidence that it is better to predict what your customers need rather than what they currently understand they want based on their current paradigm. Although Ford might not have actually said this, the point is still valid: How can people be expected to communicate that they want a car when a horse is all they know?

This is a relevant argument for revolutionary breakthroughs but perhaps less so for evolutionary improvements—where the customer is well aware of what is working well and what is not. In those cases, it is probably best to do diligent market research and closely listen to people's opinions. In fact, I would argue that even if you are aiming to metaphorically replace the customers' horses with cars, you should still research customers' opinions about their current circumstances in order to arrive at the right revolutionary solution. I've found that when you ask the proper questions, the customer actually is right, most of the time.

KANO analysis is an excellent method for researching what customers want. Professor Noriako Kano developed the *Kano model of customer satisfaction* in the 1980s. Product managers use it to analyse their requirements, or product backlogs, in order to develop a strategy for iterative, incremental development. The model involves asking potential (or in some cases existing) users of the functionality how they would feel about the potential inclusion or exclusion of potential features. The responses are then categorised according to five qualities: Must, Linear (or "One Directional"), Attractive, Indifferent, and Reverse.

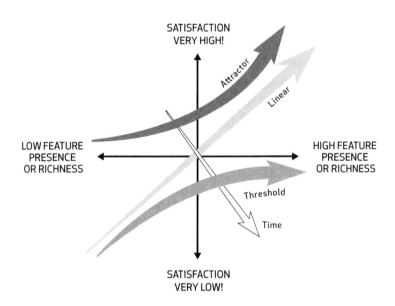

Figure I-1. A Kano Model is one method for researching what customer's want.

Requirements that fall into the ***must*** category are usually deemed threshold or mandatory features. Customers expect these features to be there; customers aren't particularly satisfied by their presence but are very sensitive to their exclusion. For example, if I were to purchase a stay in a hotel, I wouldn't be impressed to see a bed in the room (I would expect it to be there) but if there were nowhere for me to sleep then I would be incredibly dissatisfied. Therefore, the presence of a bed would be classified as a threshold feature. Focusing solely on threshold features, however, will not lead to customer satisfaction.

Linear features are also often referred to as *one-dimensional* features. They can be best described as "the more of this feature you have, the more satisfied the customer is." To use the hotel room example again, the bigger the bed I have and the more comfortable it is, the more satisfied I am going to be. Therefore, bed size and bed comfort are two linear features. With the threshold features covered and enough linear features, the model suggests that a product can achieve positive customer satisfaction.

The third main category of requirements in the Kano model is called the **attractors**, or *exciters*. These are features that the users are not expecting, perhaps didn't even consider as options, yet leave them feeling incredibly satisfied. Should these features not be present, there is no negative impact on customer satisfaction, as the customers weren't expecting them in the first place. To return to the hotel example again, receiving a complimentary bottle of wine or box of chocolates would likely excite a customer, and thus could classify as an attractor. Attractors can have such a positive effect on the customer that they may even be willing to ignore one or two missing threshold features. One note to be aware of here, though, is that exciter features can migrate very quickly into the threshold category. The next time I check in, I could well expect that bottle of wine or box of chocolates!

Indifferent features are those that are neither expected, satisfying, exciting, nor detracting. The customer doesn't care if these features are present or not. These are features that could easily be eliminated, because they have little or no impact on customer satisfaction. For example, when I check in to my hotel room, I am completely indifferent to a message on the TV that says, "Welcome, Geoff."

Last but not least, *reverse* requirements are of interest to product owners because they indicate that there is a point at which there becomes "too much of a good thing" for some users. For example, I may like the fact that there is a tablet in my hotel room that allows me to operate the lighting but if that tablet controls everything and I struggle to understand how to use it then I may soon get frustrated and long for a traditional light switch.

The Kano model uses a simple customer survey model to determine which category a requirement fits into. People are asked a functional and a dysfunctional question for each potential requirement or feature and their responses are mapped on to the following grid

Functional question: How would you feel if this feature were present?

Dysfunctional question: How would you feel if this feature were not present?

For example, if someone answered "I would like it if it were present" and "I would dislike it if it were not present" then this feature would be categorised as linear.

		DYSFUNCTIONAL				
		Like it	Expect it	Neutral	Live with	Dislike it
FUNCTIONAL	Like it	Q	A	A	A	L
	Expect it	R	Q	I	I	M
	Neutral	R	I	I	I	M
	Live with	R	I	I	Q	M
	Dislike it	R	R	R	R	Q

M Must have
R Reverse
L Linear
Q Questionable
A Attractive
I Indifferent

Figure I-2. Use the Kano Model to categorise potential features.

What message have people been trying to tell you about the product that you have so far ignored?

Observe the Customers

Even though the Kano model can help show you what your customers believe they want, it shouldn't be your sole gauge of customer interest. After all, as American anthropologist Margaret Mead famously said, "What people say, what people do, and what they say they do are entirely different things."

In other words, knowing you *should* want something doesn't always translate into actually wanting something enough to purchase it. In fact, I can think of several products where all the data has pointed towards a successful product but it has not sold. Take for example, Equator, an alcohol-free, sugar-free beer that launched in 2012.

I spoke with Karen Salters, Managing Director at Beverage Brands in the UK about the Equator product launch. Karen told me that during a focus group to test the market, the majority of customers indicated that they desired a zero-calorie, zero-sugar beer. The government, who had been searching for ways to tackle alcohol issues, were also in favour of a healthier beer. In addition, surveys demonstrated significant social support for a less filling alcohol alternative. Everything was pointing towards a product that was going to be big. When it came to it though, customers didn't buy it. Everyone knew they *should* want it, but that wasn't enough. They didn't *want* to want it. The product was not a success.

"Research tells you facts but it doesn't tell you anything behind the facts," Karen explained to me. In the successful launches of her other brands, she supplemented focus groups and surveys with observations of actual customer behavior. Then, she got feedback from the people who demonstrated that they *didn't* want the product and used that information to address the issues surrounding motivation of her customers.

If your product were a living, talking entity, what would it say to you right now?

In this chapter's story, Mike spent a bit of time observing Linda and her team working with the new features that had been developed. In doing so, he noticed that their actions did not match their feedback in previous sprint reviews. This was largely a pragmatic and political decision on the part of Linda and her team but there are many other reasons why people may not do what they say they do, especially when they don't realise they are being observed!

I'm not suggesting you surreptitiously spy on people but gathering insights into actual behavior rather than stated behavior or desired behavior can be incredibly enlightening. As Roman Pichler once told me: "Customer feedback is the basis for ideas. Customer data is the basis for decisions." A few years back, for example, I did some work with King.com, developers of mobile games such as Candy Crush Saga. They told me that they determine which products to build based on real-life user data. They fill a website with prototype games and invite their user base to play them for free. Then, rather than ask for ratings or feedback, they monitor actual usage. They track vast amounts of data about usage—the results tell them which games are the most playable, wanted, and profitable. That being said, gathering data can also be as simple as A-B testing, where you present different versions of a user interaction to 50 percent of the audience and then measure which one proves more favourable or successful.

However you choose to collect data on actual user behaviour, whether it is formal or informal, elaborate or simple, remember to trust what your customers say they want only to a point—you won't know what they actually need until you see them in action.

Develop a Clear Picture

One way to see how your customers will use your product is through the use of lo-fi objects such as paper prototypes: physical artefacts that users can manipulate in order to better demonstrate how their work gets done. Often, paper prototyping involves sketching out how a user may experience and interact with some functionality.

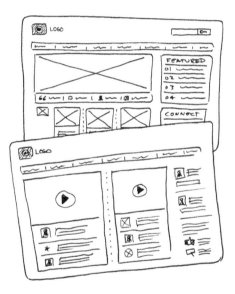

Figure I-3. Paper prototypes offer users a way to interact with something tangible.

In the story, Stef created paper prototypes to quickly test assumptions and arrive at a common understanding of what the team needed and what might be possible to develop. Stef then took the paper prototypes and the learning from the process and turned them into a really basic form of working software—nothing with any real data behind it, but just a few basic screens that mimicked the functionality of the prototypes. He then checked in with the users again, showing them the electronic versions to get more feedback and guidance before iterating again.

When your customer is having difficulty describing (or you are having difficulty understanding) a desired piece of functionality, a picture can truly be worth a thousand words. Great product owners use lo-fi tools such as paper prototypes to help them communicate more effectively with their users and customers.

Keep Failing Fast

No matter how much they might plan for success, great product owners are also always thinking about how to minimise risks if the product fails. They share a similar mantra:

"If the product is going to fail, then I would rather it fail in month 2 than month 22"

That doesn't mean that product owners plan for failure or sabotage their products. Not at all! What it does mean is that great product owners realise that time is money. Therefore, if there is a flaw in the product, they would rather find it early when there is more time to potentially deal with it or, in the worst case scenario, stop the product development effort before too much money is wasted.

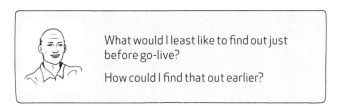

What would I least like to find out just before go-live?

How could I find that out earlier?

In the earlier story, Mike took a knock to his confidence when he mis-interpreted a couple of requirements. He felt that the right response was to make fewer assumptions—to rely more on observation and data than he had been doing. Please note, though, that the key words in that response is *fewer* and *more*. When product owners make one or two bad decisions, they can overcorrect, swerving too far in the other direction, over-thinking each feature. Mike had plenty of evidence in the months before that his intuition and analysis were reasonably accurate, so he shouldn't abandon them altogether. Although gathering data, asking questions, and observing customers is important, it is far better to develop the wrong thing quickly and get feedback than to wait around too long in an attempt to ensure that no mistakes are ever made. Great product owners know how to find the right middle ground, one with an appropriate balance of data and intuition—and a good measure of courage.

"So. If there were no pressure whatsoever,
what would you suggest then?"

Question and Answer

Good product owners know enough to make decisions.
Great product owners know enough to ask questions.

Judy was pleased with how the sprint review meeting had gone and was looking forward to the next part of the day, when she and the rest of the team would plan their next sprint. She had already explained how they were going to focus this upcoming sprint on expanding the artificial intelligence functionality. She'd even come up with an enticing sprint goal, labeling it The Turing Sprint in honor of Alan Turing, widely considered to be the father of theoretical computer science and artificial intelligence. She could sense an almost tangible anticipation among the stakeholders and development team members of finally getting to build some of the sexy new features.

As had become the norm in sprint planning meetings, Judy began the second half of the meeting by re-iterating the goal of the sprint that she had first mentioned in that morning's meeting and posting up on the walls some large printouts of the highest priority features. These printouts, which she and the team had created during one of their frequent "product backlog refinement workshops," not only contained the user stories and acceptance criteria but also some user journeys explaining how this functionality would eliminate one or more problems that the user community were facing.

Next, Judy and the development team began working through a number of the technical implementation details, creating a sprint backlog for the next couple of weeks. One of the stories proved a little more challenging than the others though.

"This one is tricky to plan out. It all depends on how we approach it. How do you want us to do it?" asked Ceri, one of the developers.

"As you know I'm not the expert in these things. What do you think my options are?" replied Judy.

"Sounds like a great opportunity for a Brainstorm Battle!" suggested Lee, the ScrumMaster.

"Great idea" agreed Judy.

Judy left the room to get some much needed coffee while the team broke into four groups. Each group began to "battle" in a Brainstorm Battle, a fun collaborative exercise to help bring out multiple ideas and provide a fun structure for them to analyse and filter them. By the end of the battle, the team had narrowed the options down to two, which they presented to Judy.

Though they did a thorough job in explaining each option, the team didn't seem as excited as they usually were after one of their Brainstorm Battles. Judy waited for more ideas to come forth, but the team was silent.

"Both options sound like they would work," Judy began. "But something doesn't quite feel right."

Out of the corner of her eye, Judy happened to notice one of the developers, Suzanne, silently nodding her agreement but otherwise remaining quiet—much quieter, Judy realised, than she normally was.

Judy paused for a moment, then said, "I'm still not sure I know enough yet to make this decision. I'd be really interested to hear what some of you would do if you were in my shoes, though." She turned to Suzanne and asked, "What are your thoughts, Suzanne?"

Suzanne looked up, startled, but answered quickly. "To be honest, I think we're under a little bit too much pressure and this might be affecting our approach. I don't truly believe either of those options are going to be a strategic solution. I'm concerned that we are looking to make a decision too quickly simply because we are in a timeboxed sprint planning session."

"Interesting. I understand what you mean." Judy said. "So. If there were no pressure whatsoever; if nobody minded if we didn't find a solution during this meeting or even implement this functionality during this particular sprint, what would you suggest then?"

Suzanne cocked her head and looked up to her left as she pondered what Judy had asked, then said, "That's an intriguing question. If I had all the time in the world, given the state of our architecture and some of the decisions we have made in the past, I would recommend we pick apart some of the work we did last sprint. A few existing features probably need to be redesigned to accommodate this particular feature more strategically." Suzanne then went on to describe in detail some of the decisions they had made in the past and how a few tweaks would make the AI functionality work better in the long run.

"Thanks for speaking up," said Judy. "I know you wouldn't suggest that lightly. And, although I admit it sounds risky because the existing features have already been signed off and seen by the stakeholders, I can definitely see the logic there. What does everyone else think?"

Ceri was the first to answer: "I think that Suzanne's suggestion would be immensely beneficial. But it would probably increase the cost by about 50 percent."

The rest of the team murmured their agreement.

"Ouch. That's an expensive proposition," Judy replied. "Even if I agree to this, it's going to be a tough sell for the stakeholders." She paused for a moment then asked the team a different question: "If you were paying for this, what would make it a more attractive deal?"

The team looked at each other thoughtfully for a minute or two. Finally, Lee said "Perhaps we could fix a few items of technical debt at the same time. That would be a sweeter proposition."

"I like the sound of that," Judy said as she pulled out the list of technical debt.

Ceri, Suzanne and the others then picked out 4 integration issues that they had noticed which all related in some way to the features they'd be reworking. They showed Judy how they could fix them at the same time as they were redesigning the features from last sprint. This added extra benefit to the sprint, making it much more palatable.

Once the technical debt items were chosen and the redesign of the features planned out, Judy looked down at all of the fancy new features she'd been hoping to implement this sprint—features that would have to wait now until a future sprint.

"I want to thank you for speaking up. I have to tell you that it's not what I wanted to hear—at all. The stakeholders and I were so excited for this sprint and seeing all the new features come to life—and I know you were too. But I can see the logic behind approaching this more strategically and I agree that it's the right thing to do," Judy admitted. "Maybe before I take this back to the stakeholders, we should rename our sprint goal. How about "Bite the Bullet?" It's not as exciting as "The Turing Sprint" but it's reflective of our commitment to do the tough things now in order to reap the rewards later. I think it might help convince them to be patient just a bit longer.

The team agreed. Judy took great care to explain the logic behind the decision to the stakeholders and went out of her way to keep them informed of progress throughout the sprint. As a result, their initial apprehension soon gave way to confidence in the decision to invest in a long-term solution.

Question What Isn't Being Said

Good product owners know about the product and its market. And most product owners are aware of their responsibilities in that regard. Truly informed product owners, however, have that same level of knowledge about people. That's why great product owners pay close attention both to what the people they are working with are doing and saying and also to what they are not doing and not saying.

In the story, Judy was able to hear not only what the team was saying:

"Here are two options to consider"

She was also able to hear what they were not saying:

"We don't particularly think either option will work well."

How? By observing the team's behaviour closely, by asking probing questions, and by listening carefully to their response.

> How well do you know your team?
>
> How would knowing your team better be helpful to you, them and the product?

Please don't misinterpret my exhortation to pay attention to mean interrogating people or doubting their answers. I have met some product owners who feel they must bombard the team with questions about the technical side of things–not because the product owners are especially interested in the answers but because they are afraid of getting bamboozled or taken advantage of. I do not recommend those kinds of questions. What I do recommend are what I refer to as CHILD questions, so called because they share a number of key characteristics that just so happen to spell out CHILD. Great product owners ask questions that are **c**urious, **h**umble, **i**lluminating, **l**imitless, and **d**irect.

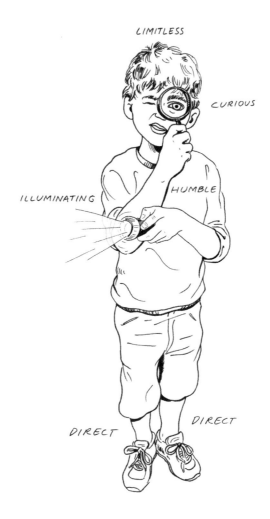

Stay Curious

Good product owners are curious—both about the product and also about the people working on it. Their questions arise from a genuine desire to understand, and as such are engaging and thought provoking. More often than not, this kind of curiosity is contagious.

Soon, others also begin exploring the deeper levels of the topic in hand (or themselves).

Being curious, however, is no good unless you actually listen to the answer. To paraphrase *Stephen Covey*, most people listen with the intent to reply. Great product owners, however, sincerely want to know what other people think; they haven't already got an answer in mind. One simple technique to demonstrate that you have listened to someone's answer is to play back what you heard them say rather than immediately follow up with an opinion of your own.

Great product owners are curious about the environment that their product is in and enjoy learning. They set time aside every week, sometimes every day, to learn more and indulge their curiosity about the product, the market, the users and the team. Great product owners are also curious about what is going on around them and their own behaviours. They learn to notice when they are not listening, or listening superficially, or when they are asking for the sake of being nosy – some product owners even ask others to hold them accountable on these bad habits in order to focus and sharpen their curiosity in the right way.

In the story earlier, Judy noticed just from observing Suzanne's body language that she seemed to have reservations but hadn't yet voiced them. She invited Suzanne to share her thoughts and was rewarded with information she had not considered. Being interested and curious is powerful.

I find that questions that begin with "I wonder why…" or "What if…?" or "Isn't it interesting that…?" often imply a healthy curiosity.

Remain Humble

As I discussed earlier, good product owners know when to trust the experts and don't feel the need to figure everything out themselves. They are comfortable with the fact that they don't know everything, and feel secure just knowing others who do. They are confidently **humble**. And as such, tend to generate much greater levels of rapport than people who are arrogant or insecure.

Questions that demonstrate humility are well received as they show vulnerability and they avoid making people defensive or uncomfortable. People recognize that questions asked out of a true desire to understand aren't about scoring points or stealing ideas. Asking humble questions also models a behaviour for others in the team, encouraging them to embrace vulnerability, ask for help more, and not try to always put a brave face on or pretend they know when they don't.

Great product owners know the strength of humility, which is why they go out of their way to assign credit where it is due (even if they did know that anyway) and why they consciously avoid games of one-upmanship, where they follow a suggestion with one of their own that they think is better (even if they can make that idea better).

I find questions that begin with "I don't know, what do you think…?" or "I'm not the expert here…" or "I'd love to get your view on…" often imply a healthy humility.

Illuminate the Situation

Great product owners have a habit of asking questions that **illuminate** the situation for themselves and others. These questions can shine a light on new options or hidden constraints. They can even help connect the dots to identify patterns, causality, or perhaps the ultimate source of a problem or solution.

In the story, Judy asks the team, "If you were paying for the sprint, what would make it more attractive?" This leads the team to consider the problem from a new point of view and to suggest that perhaps fixing technical debt while reworking features would make the investment more palatable to the stakeholders.

Good product owners ask questions that help others see new things and find new ways to tackle tricky problems. Great product owners ask questions designed to give others the tools and space to come up with creative solutions rather than just impose a solution upon them.

I find questions that begin with "So is there a connection between…?" or "What does this tell us about that…?" or "What does it mean that…?" often offer illumination.

Encourage Limitless Thinking

People tend to think about situations from within their own paradigm. Everyone has a view of the world and a whole load of unconscious assumptions. Assumptions about what the problem is, what the available options are, which skills and knowledge currently exist, what is logical, even about what is true and factual.

Great product owners attempt to shatter these assumptions by suspending disbelief and embracing the hypothetical, the impossible, and the sometimes downright ludicrous. They challenge their own constraints and assumptions and encourage others to do so by asking **limitless** questions—questions that transcend the limits we assume exist.

Returning again to the story, Judy asked Suzanne a question that gave her permission to consider options that she might have thought were off the table when she asked, "So. If there were no pressure whatsoever ... what would you suggest then?"

As well as encouraging people to challenge the limits of the situation, great product owners also tend to encourage people to challenge their own limits (both individually and as a team) and demonstrate a genuine belief in the potential of those around to answer a question or solve a problem.

I find questions that begin with "If we could do anything...?" or "If we were actually better than we thought we are...? Or "If we were wrong about everything...?" often imply a healthy questioning of reality and its current limits.

Be Direct

Direct questions are honest, straightforward, and to the point. They hide no ulterior motives and convey only interest, not suspicion. The straightforwardness and sincerity of a direct question breaks down barriers and opens up dialog. In this way, direct questions—ones that are not hiding any agenda and are exactly what they appear to be—build trust and rapport.

Great product owners are cautious, though, about when and how they ask questions. They look for context clues and notice non-verbal clues, like body language. They are careful always not to confuse being direct for being blunt, disrespectful, or putting someone under pressure.

When Judy noticed Suzanne was quieter than normal she asked her directly for her thoughts. Her question hid no threats or accusations, but instead reflected her genuine interest in what she keenly perceived as some reservations on Suzanne's part about the options being presented. This, coupled with the trust Judy had already established with Suzanne and the rest of the team in the preceding sprints, gave Suzanne the confidence to be just as direct in her answer.

Great product owners find ways to build a little more CHILD into their listening and questioning techniques by asking questions that are curious, humble, illuminating, limitless, and direct. In doing so, they become better informed and better able to make the right decision for their products.

How could you make the questions you ask the team more effective?

Make Time for Answers

To enable effective decisions to be made, great product owners take the time to ensure that both they, the rest of the team, and if possible the other stakeholders are as informed as possible. The earlier story mentions two techniques for sharing knowledge amongst the team: product backlog refinement workshops and brainstorm battles.

A **product backlog refinement workshop** is a collaborative meeting that happens typically once every sprint. During the workshop, the product owner and members of the development team (and sometimes other stakeholders) get together to explore some of the upcoming high-priority items on the product backlog.

Product backlog refinement workshops do not have an industry-standard agenda—they are intended to be an optional and adaptable part of an agile product management framework. However, most agile teams are relatively consistent on a number of factors when incorporating these workshops into their working practices.

Product backlog refinement workshops typically take place about a bit more than halfway through the iteration and usually last no less than 30 minutes and no more than 2 hours. During these workshops, the team have the opportunity to clarify the user story details and ask questions about edge cases and "what if…" scenarios that will help them when they come to plan the sprint. The product owner has the opportunity to take note of any questions that can't be answered during the workshop and to research specific information that the team need prior to the sprint planning meeting.

Holding regular product backlog refinement workshops tends to make sprint planning smoother and more effective. The team come into the meeting with a good understanding of the high priority features and are therefore able to estimate them much more confidently and quickly. The team are also able to avoid situations where they have to reject any high-priority features because of missing information. As described in the story, the artefacts from the workshops can even become part of the sprint planning meeting, helping to make that meeting more tactile, visual, and engaging. For these reasons, product backlog refinement workshops are worth the time and effort teams and product owners invest in them.

A **Brainstorm Battle** is another way teams share information. A brainstorm battle is a creative problem solving and analysis technique I have used with a number of teams to help them collaboratively consider, critique and compare alternative ways to address a situation.

The structure can be tailored based on the number of people present and the number of options available to consider but follows the basic process below:

1. State the problem and any constraints that must be met or abided by. Remind the team to challenge any assumptions—to ask, Is this truly essential? Is that really set in stone?

2. Split into 4 groups (try to ensure that each group consists of at least 2 people). For no more than 30 minutes, have each group work independently to identify potential options to address the problem in step 1. You may wish to encourage each group to identify multiple options and rank them internally.

3. When the timebox ends, groups 1 and 2 will take turns presenting their proposed options to groups 3 and 4.

4. After both groups 1 and 2 have presented their options, groups 3 and 4 will vote on which option they prefer. The winning option will go through to the next round. As an example, let's assume groups 3 & 4 preferred the Group 1 option.

5. Groups 3 and 4 will then have an opportunity to present their options to groups 1 and 2, who will vote for their preferred option amongst the options presented by groups 3 and 4. Again, the winning option goes through to the next round. This time, let's assume, that groups 1 & 2 chose the option put forward by Group 3.

6. Ideally there will be a small timebox where the whole group can offer feedback on the two winning options. The winning groups, in this example, groups 1 and 3, get an extra 10 minutes to incorporate that feedback and improve their proposals for the next round, at which time the losing groups (groups 2 and 4) vote on which of the revised options they prefer.

There are many ways that this basic structure can be altered to meet the context of the team. Teams can argue each option against each of the others; they also can narrow down all of the options only to two (or three) and present multiple options to a decision-maker, as described in the story.

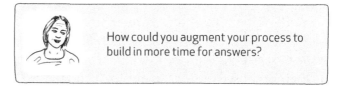

How could you augment your process to build in more time for answers?

Regardless of whether they use these techniques or some other tool, great product owners are acutely aware that the team – and other stakeholders – have a wealth of knowledge and experience. When faced with a difficult decision, especially when it is unclear whether there is a "right" answer, great product owners make time for the open and collaborative sharing and critiquing of information in order to make the best decision possible.

Stay Informed

Good product owners are well informed. They know it isn't enough just to create a product backlog and show up at all of the right meetings. Instead, they understand that being available and accessible to their teams means being able to quickly solicit, elicit, and process enough information to make timely decisions.

Part of being well informed is understanding the product space, the market environment, and the potential purchasers, consumers, and users of their product. By balancing information gathering with the fast feedback and learning opportunities that come from using an agile process, great product owners make decisions that position their products for success.

Being well informed has another, perhaps less obvious, aspect: understanding others well enough to ask the right questions, of the right people, at the right time and knowing yourself well enough to accept and act on the answers. Great product owners create opportunities for people to find and share the breakthrough ideas that hide behind real or perceived constraints.

Product owners who are well informed in both aspects—products and people—are able to make the decisions necessary to bring the right product to market at the right time.

DRIVEN

Versatile

"In matters of style, swim with the tide.
In matters of principle, stand like a rock."
Thomas Jefferson

One truth that DRIVEN product owners learn early on, is that agile teams operate in an environment of complexity, uncertainty and change – three factors that increase fear and stress within human beings. That's one reason why, amid the chaos that surrounds any creative endeavor, good product owners strive to be resolute, confident, and determined in making decisions and choosing a path forward. They know that being decisive, somewhat ruthless, and always well informed helps to minimise their teams' anxiety so they can focus on the work at hand.

Great product owners, however, understand how easily those desirable traits, if taken to the extreme, can mutate into being rigid, stubborn, and unyielding. As such, great product owners are also DRIVEN to be flexible and **versatile**, able to adapt in a volatile environment. Great product owners strive to be self-assured without being dogmatic or inflexible; they realize that they can never know everything and are open to changing course based on feedback, new information or data.

The stories and discussion that follow illustrate how great product owners learn exactly how to display the seeming contradiction of standing strong by being versatile, both in their dealings with the team and also in their plans for the product they are developing.

Alex was feeling a little nervous. She hadn't worked with this team before and was keen to make a good impression

After Alex goes home,
the team carry on drinking

Bend and Stand Firm

A good product owner is reliable and dependable.
A great product owner knows flexibility is essential
for strength.

It was a classic British summer's day; the sun was threatening to come out but stubbornly refusing. Instead it hid behind the clouds and even forced a few drops of rain from them. Alex, the product owner, had organized a team barbeque after managing to find a little bit of budget for the food and drink. When questioned about the time out of office and the expense of the meal, she had made the case that if she and the team all got on outside of work then they would get on inside of work and deliver better results.

The team were certainly enjoying it, regardless of the somewhat lacklustre August weather; perhaps the free beer had something to do with it! Alex herself, though, was feeling a little nervous; worried that the weather might turn, that they might run out of beer, that the music wasn't right, and so on. She was keen to make a good impression and well aware of the reputation that product owners had in this company—that they relied on their authority to push for unrealistic deadlines. She wanted to prove she could be approachable and adaptable, while still accomplishing the goals for the sprint.

They were a few sprints into this delivery and this was their second team social event. So far, things seemed to be going reasonably well. They'd made a few mistakes, but as far as Alex could tell the team were working well and happy with the project. In fact one of the team members, Polly, had come up to Alex unsolicited to tell her that this was probably the best team spirit she had seen at the company. "Even, when the team had that dodgy second sprint where we hardly managed to complete anything." Polly added in a conspiratorial tone. Polly put the fact that the team rebounded so well down to the fact that Alex hadn't reacted angrily like all the other product owners would have done.

At 8 pm, the party showed no signs of slowing down. Alex decided it was time to say her goodbyes. She was already growing anxious about tomorrow's meeting with one of their key stakeholders, Ted. She had specifically asked Ted, who had been openly critical about the "dodgy second sprint" Polly had mentioned, to travel to meet with her and the team for two reasons. Firstly, she hoped he would be reassured by seeing the progress the team had made since those early sprints. Secondly, she felt that Ted was the ideal person to help the team find the answers to a couple of questions they had with the current sprint. She wanted it all to go well.

Alex decided that the best way to quit worrying about the meeting was to get a good night's sleep. The team waved enthusiastically as she left, thanking her again for organising such a great team event. Alex smiled and headed home, feeling much better about her relationship with the team and cautiously optimistic about the stakeholder meeting.

The next morning, Alex's good mood was spoiled by an unexpected visit from a visibly annoyed Ted. He reported that after traveling some distance specifically to meet with the team, they had sent an email early that morning asking to postpone because they needed more time to finish some of the features and bug fixes they had planned to demonstrate. Alex knew this was a complete fabrication—she'd seen all of that functionality working just yesterday. She suspected, based on how several members of the team had looked as she passed through the team space earlier that morning, that the real reason for the postponement was that the team wasn't fit for work after their late night at the party.

Alex apologised profusely to Ted and suggested a number of other things they could do together while he was in the office so that trip wouldn't be a total waste. After he left, she sat in her office seething with anger and riddled with indecision. Not only had the team's delay upset an already apprehensive stakeholder but it had also put the sprint goal in jeopardy. Today's meeting had been intended to illuminate a number of risks and dependencies—those conversations, and the features they informed, would now have to wait for the rescheduled meeting.

For Alex, though, even worse than all that was the damage the team had done to their relationship. How could she ever trust the team again? Yet what kind of damage would it do to their good rapport if she expressed her frustration? She supposed that she could just shrug off the team's lie, since Ted had believed it. Yet as much as her people-pleaser instinct wanted her to do otherwise, Alex knew that she couldn't just sweep the team's behaviour under the rug. She reminded herself that there's a time to be flexible, such as when the team had missed its sprint goal in sprint 2, and a time to be firm, such as the team cancelling a meeting with a key stakeholder because they are too hung over to participate! Alex pounded a fist on her desk determinedly—Yes, she thought to herself, this was completely unacceptable and set a dangerous precedent. She let go of her doubts and began to prepare herself for an important, yet difficult conversation.

Be Strong by Being Flexible

There's an old African proverb that says, "The wind does not break a tree that bends." Alex demonstrated quite a bit of tree-like flexibility in this story—but not just in the ways that are obvious.

Clearly Alex's friendliness, empathy, and easy-going nature had quickly earned her a bond of trust with the development team. The team felt comfortable laughing and joking with her as well as socialising with her. These same personality traits had also helped to dispel the notion that all the product owners at her company were taskmasters, with no understanding of the realities of developing in an uncertain environment.

Alex had set firm sprint goals but had been flexible and understanding when the team had failed to meet them. She had also reached out to stakeholders (such as Ted) to help set their minds at ease about the team's progress and also to help remove some of the uncertainty that was blocking the team from completing their work. With all of these actions, Alex had proven herself to be a good product owner. She was determined but not stubborn; resolute but not rigid.

But the strongest display of Alex's ability to adapt came when her innate tendencies to please others and be accommodating came into conflict with the good of the project as a whole. She knew the team had crossed a line by cancelling the stakeholder meeting, and was concerned that holding them to account would damage the still-fragile relationship she had built with them.

It would have been much easier for her to just sweep the problem under the rug and move on. But Alex didn't choose the easy path. She understood that great product owners must stand firm when it comes to defending principles such as trust and respect. Somewhat ironically, Alex stood her ground by being even more flexible and versatile—in other words, she deviated from her natural leadership style in order to confront the situation. Let's look more closely at what it means to be strong on principles by being versatile in style.

How important is it to you that people like you?

How does that impact your work?

Adapt Your Leadership Style to the Context

Good product owners have a consistent leadership style; one the team can depend on from day to day. Great product owners, however, also learn how to adapt their preferred style to fit the situation at hand. In his book *Primal Leadership: Unleashing The Power of Emotional Intelligence*, Daniel Goleman explains that there is no "right" or "best" leadership style but rather that the most effective leaders are versatile: they are able to navigate across a range of leadership styles depending on the circumstances they are facing. Everyone, however, is likely to have a default or preferred leadership style, and so being aware of this is a useful first step.

Figure V-1 below shows six leadership styles, as identified by Goleman: affiliative, coercive, pace-setting, democratic, visionary and coaching. Leaders that adopt an **affiliative** leadership style focus more on building up relationships within their team, ensuring morale is high and stress is low. They are prepared to sacrifice a certain amount of focus on the task and team performance in order to achieve harmony. While immediate performance may suffer as a result of adopting an affiliative leadership style, the extra benefits gained from developing the team spirit and raising morale often pay dividends in the medium-to-long term as affiliative leaders often find that teams "go the extra mile" for them when it's really needed. A **coercive** style, on the other hand, is often appropriate in times of crisis and when poor performance needs to be addressed. This leadership style can be summed up by the phrase "do as I say" and is focused on obtaining immediate compliance.

If the coercive leadership style is summed up by the phrase "do as I say," the **pace-setting** leadership style is summed up by the phrase "do as I do" and is built upon the premise of a leader who leads by example. The pace-setting leader sets high standards for performance, demonstrates meeting them and then expects those around them to meet them as well.

Teams with pace-setting leaders often experience short-term boosts to productivity and have little ambiguity about what is expected of one another. If the team is highly skilled and able to reach the standards set by the leader then great results, high levels of quality and conscientiousness can be achieved, and quickly, by adopting this style. However, a pace-setting leadership style is just as likely to demotivate those who aren't equipped or who lack confidence. In fact, it is often cited as a reason behind burnout in the workplace as people struggle to maintain the pace set by the leader for even moderate amounts of time. Leaders adopting this style also tend to suffer more from stress and burnout issues.

The other leadership styles mentioned by Goleman are **democratic,** where the leader focuses on gaining participation and consensus, **visionary** (sometimes called *authoritative*) where the leader attempts to mobilise people towards a vision and asks them to "come with me", and **coaching,** where the leader focuses on developing people's potential, self-awareness and empathy even at the expense of imme-diate results by encouraging people to "try this".

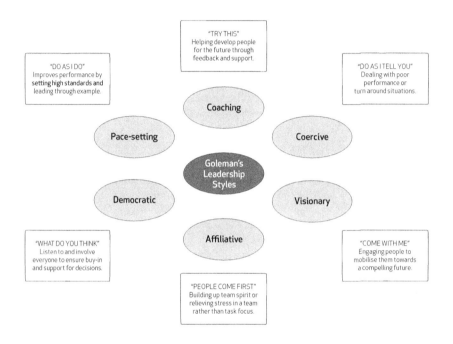

Figure V-1. Good product owners are aware of their preferred leadership style.

In the story, Alex had a consistent leadership style: *affiliative*. Alex realised, however, that in order to hold the team accountable for canceling the stakeholder meeting, she was going to have to tem-porarily adopt a more *coercive* leadership style. Figure V-2 offers examples of when it might be appropriate for a product owner to be versatile by temporarily adopting a style outside their preferred one.

Leadership Style	When a Product Owner might adopt it
Coercive	To take remedial action or make an urgent decision, such as whether a feature needs to be redone as it has failed to meet quality standards.
Affiliative	To build up the team spirit within the development team or product owner team and to develop rapport with stakeholders or third parties.
Visionary	To generate enthusiasm and engagement at the beginning of the product development effort, an iteration or release, or perhaps to reignite momentum after a flat period.
Coaching	When the team is flexing its self-organisation muscles and is making a few minor imperfect decisions. Doing so will help the development team become more comfortable with responsibility and pro-activeness.
Pace-setting	When highly skilled, motivated and experienced colleagues or teams already possess the tools necessary for self-management and self-analysis and are craving a role model to follow.
Democratic	To increase engagement and buy-in to the decision-making process or product development direction, especially when there isn't one clear answer.

Figure V-2. Great product owners adapt their leadership style to the context.

Which leadership style do you tend to find most difficult to adopt?

What would make it easier for you?

Approach Difficult Conversations Confidently

In the story, Alex decided to adopt a more coercive leadership style, which meant engaging the team in a difficult conversation about trust and expectations. Difficult conversations don't have to be damaging to relationships. In fact, done correctly, they can open channels of communication and actually improve rapport. In their book *Crucial Conversations: Tools for Talking when Stakes are High*, authors Patterson, Grenny, McMillan & Switzler recommend that in difficult conversations, each person should STATE their story:

Share your facts
Tell your story
Ask for others paths
Talk tentatively
Encourage testing

First, **share** the facts of what has occurred. By beginning with facts, there is a greater chance for alignment around objective aspects of the situation. It is less likely that people will disagree that a set of events happened – the disagreement is more likely around how the events were intended or interpreted. The more agreement and alignment people can reach early on, the more chance they have of reaching a mutually beneficial outcome.

For example, Alex could share all of the following objective facts with the team:

- The team postponed the stakeholder meeting.
- The stakeholder had travelled down specifically for that meeting.
- The stakeholder expressed his disappointment to Alex.

These facts carry no explicit judgement; and, indeed, it is important to remove as much judgement as possible from this part of the process to avoid premature defensiveness.

After sharing the facts, **tell** the story of how the events affected you. When telling your story, own your statements and interpretations but talk tentatively: Tell your side of the story *as a story* rather than a fact. Talking tentatively does not mean having no conviction in what you say but it does mean avoiding extreme or inflammatory language. For example, instead of saying "It's obvious that…" think about saying "I'm beginning to wonder if…" Carefully choosing the language with which we tell our stories ensures that we avoid claiming something as factual when it is merely an opinion. For example, Alex should probably relay to the team that she felt embarrassed to have to cover for them with the stakeholder and felt they let her down and took advantage of her trust. While the team may disagree that they would have felt the same, they should be able to acknowledge Alex's right to those feelings.

Great product owners are humble enough to realise that they don't have all the facts and that there are multiple ways to interpret an event. After telling your story, **ask** for others' paths. All involved are entitled to explain how they saw things and how they were impacted. While this is arguable in its objectivity, it is fair for people to express however they felt about the event. This should be encouraged and respected; therefore, actively invite others to tell the story of how they interpret the situation and what they are thinking and feeling. For example, Alex could explain that she saw the postponement of the meeting as a direct result of the team members being hungover but might also concede that there are other possible reasons for the meeting to have been postponed. She could invite the team to explain those reasons. She might also mention the negative consequences that she fears may result from this and then ask the team what consequences they perceive as possible.

The last thing to remember is to **encourage** testing of your opinions, which means purposefully inviting others to play devil's advocate, to poke holes in your theories and challenge your thinking. As the authors rightly point out in *Crucial Conversations*, "the only limit to how strongly you can express your opinion is your willingness to encourage others to challenge it" (134). Asking "What am I missing here?" or "What if I'm completely wrong?" brings people into the dialogue and introduces perspectives that might otherwise be missing from the conversation.

There will undoubtedly be times when, as a product owner, you will need to have a difficult conversation—one that involves conflict and stirs emotions but that needs to be had for the good of the product and your long-term relationship with the team

What conversations do you tend to avoid?

What would make you more comfortable having them?

Remain Flexibly Firm

Great product owners demonstrate remarkable versatility. They have discovered that in a chaotic and uncertain environment, they can control one variable more than others – themselves. As such, they strive to be predictable and reliable while maintaining and improving their versatility.

Foresee and Fine-tune

Good product owners define a cohesive vision for the product.
Great product owners empirically evolve the product.

Throughout this book, I've illustrated good to great product owner-ship through fictionalised accounts of situations I've witnessed in my work. For this particular aspect of the versatility trait, however, I have permission to share with you an actual story that happened at a company called Made by Many. It's an excellent example of how product owners should be prescient enough to create a far-reaching vision for the product and versatile enough to evolve the vision based on feedback and data.

Made by Many is a digital product design studio in the UK that, according to its *website*, helps "clients take on the challenge of rapid change in markets and technologies by creating brilliantly success-ful digital products and new ventures." One of the technologies they helped create was an online educational product that enables transformative learning using video calling. Made by Many's product manager, Fiona, told me the story of a sprint review where she went in to proudly deliver a new piece of functionality for that product only to be hit by not one, but two, curveballs in the form of requests for new features.

First, a bit of background. A few years back, the client's product owner (we'll call her Alice) began hearing stories of how teachers were beginning to use their product in amazing, innovative ways. Alice engaged Made by Many to help them design and build a site to showcase these stories. When they began interviewing teachers for the project, it quickly became clear that there was a bigger opportunity available. The teachers that were using the video-calling software seemed to all share the same problem: as early adopters they were spread out across the world and struggled to find other teachers who were using the service—in other words, they couldn't figure out who to call!

In response to this feedback, Made by Many and the client came up with a game. In the game, two or more classes compete to guess each other's locations using only yes or no questions. Made by Many felt it would be a fun way for new users to get started using the software and would make it easier for teachers to find other classrooms that were using the video-calling software.

Fiona, from Made by Many, and Alice, from the client organisation, took on the product owner role together for the first release of the game. They devised a new question set for the early adopter interviews and used the information they gathered to help them form a product vision and a product roadmap. Before long, they were developing functionality. And after a few months, they were ready to release an early version to the world. Fiona expressed how much she was looking forward to that particular sprint review: "I was so excited when it came time to present the new game at the sprint review. I was sure it would be well received by the stakeholders and couldn't wait to make it available to the user community."

The sprint review seemed to be going smoothly. One of the team members briefly explained the history and concept behind the game and then demonstrated the functionality that had been developed so far. He completed his presentation with feedback from one of the teachers they had been working with during development. She had said, "This is great. This new feature has inspired me to do things I wouldn't naturally have thought of in my teaching practice."

Fiona looked at Alice and smiled, thinking of how well things had gone. She was just about to express her pleasure when one of the stakeholders spoke up instead. "I've had a chance to play around with this new game for the past couple of weeks, so I've got some fairly specific feedback," the stakeholder explained. "Overall, it's a great piece of functionality but I did notice that it adds complexity to the navigation. Plus, it doesn't integrate with search.

"And while we're on that topic, my team have been struggling with the search functionality a lot lately – it's hard to find what we're looking for – it kind of worked when we had fewer lessons and teachers to trawl through, but now I keep seeing really poor quality lessons when I try searching and can never get a precise result".

This stakeholder then went on to describe how she'd like the search functionality to be enhanced. She suggested adding extra filters, such as subjects, type of teacher, location, lesson quality, and lesson age. Fiona and the development team took notes, but Fiona couldn't help but wonder if these were the right features to work on next.

Before Fiona could comment another member of the product owner team spoke up; this time it was a representative from a third-party PR agency. He, too, praised the new functionality, but then added, "We have a great opportunity now to publicise this game on the homepage. To do that most effectively, I think we need to create some new features to showcase the game so that passing journalists will notice and download our press packages. That way we maximise news coverage."

Fiona knew that all of this feedback and the resulting feature requests were valid, but something didn't seem right. She loved sprint reviews and the opportunity it gave her to gather feedback and evolve the product based on that feedback, but these new features seemed somehow outside the scope of the game they had set out to develop. She thought to herself, "Yes, the new functionality for the homepage might attract passing journalists, but were the features really part of the game they were developing? And yes, the search functionality needed revision, but just adding some filters might not be the right solution."

While Fiona was pondering these things, Alice spoke up, "Those seem like relatively easy fixes. I'm sure we can tackle them in the next sprint."

Fiona stood up. "I agree. Those are relatively easy fixes. But before we go too far down that road, I want to revisit the product vision for this particular game. Give me just a moment, please"

Fiona dug around in her archives and found the original vision, which she projected onto the screen:

"Helping teachers who are using the video-calling software in their classrooms to find each other."

Fiona looked around the room and realised that not many of the original stakeholders were left on the project team. When the project had begun, Fiona and Alice had interviewed and observed a number of teachers in order to craft the goal of the product but, from the perspective of the new stakeholders, she could easily see how this vision would not feel expansive enough. It had also been a while since they'd done any research that looked at the whole experience of using the video-calling software in classrooms. She could see how it might be difficult for new stakeholders to make good suggestions for solutions when they didn't understand the motivations and needs of the teachers they were building for.

"I think this would be a great point to just check in with where this product is going and where we want it to go." Fiona said, pointing at the original vision statement.

"I think we can all agree that this version of the game delivers our first vision: to help teachers find each other. However, we have a range of options for where we take it moving forward. This project started as a really simple idea of connecting teachers who were trying to use the video-calling software in the classroom but it has gone way past that already."

Fiona went on to explain that part of the game's success was down to a clear, simple vision and ruthless prioritisation. The decisions they had made had been based on talking to the actual users, which had helped them focus on delivering a Minimal Viable Product quickly.

"I think we need to follow that approach again here. Although your feedback today has been very helpful, I think that rather than make guesses based on what we'd like to see ourselves, we need to reconnect with our user base to find out what *they* want next.

"Don't get me wrong: The changes to the search functionality are potentially a great investment, and the homepage changes might be too, but I'd prefer to choose what we do next based on direct evidence from the teachers," Fiona added.

Fiona then asked the stakeholders to agree to invest in one sprint's worth of research to collect the data required to determine how to improve the search functionality and better promote the new game and also how to discover exactly what teachers were experiencing in connecting with each other using the product. She explained how the original vision and product roadmap had been based on a few pioneer teachers who were already comfortable with technology – but in order to meet the client's business objectives of reaching a much larger number of classrooms and teachers, there needed to be a shift in thinking to consider how the service could help to on-board the complete novice.

She detailed how she and others would interview teachers, both ones who were using the service and ones who had never heard of it. She also proposed that the rest of the team could spend their time this sprint working on a couple of features on the backlog that she absolutely knew were important.

The stakeholders agreed. In the next sprint review, Fiona showcased the extra features the team had delivered, and then presented the findings from their research. She then led the new stakeholder group in evolving the vision into the following elevator statement:

For time- and resource-poor teachers

Who want to provide new and transformative experiences to their students

Our product is an online collaboration tool

That makes extraordinary learning experiences possible no matter the teacher's level of technological proficiency

Unlike physically bringing in guest speakers or going on expensive field trips

Every teacher can use this regardless of their budget or geographical constraints.

After a bit more discussion, the team was given the go-ahead to test the following hypothesis:

Simplifying navigation and enabling teachers to browse first will increase the number of teachers who take part in lessons they find on the service.

This was a hypothesis that Fiona could measure going forward. Over the next few sprints, the statistics showed how successful they had been in choosing new features:

- 62% increase in 'taking part', which was the indicator that teachers were actually finding something inspirational that they'd like to try in their classroom more easily.
- 71.56% increase in pages per visit
- 61.4% increase in time on site
- 5% decrease in bounce rate

What hypothesis would you like to test?

How would you know if it was successful?

Approach Blind Turns Cautiously

Sprint reviews give every product owner the opportunity to practice their versatility in terms of willingness to change course. At each sprint review, the future of the product can change dramatically based on the feedback the stakeholders provide upon seeing the latest developments. Sprint reviews, however, can also be a time for product owners to stand firm when feedback doesn't match the product vision.

Good product owners have the courage to stick to their guns when they know in their hearts—or have proven through research—that something is the right thing to do. Great product owners also have the versatility (and humility) to let go of something they once believed to be right—to change their own opinions and bend to the good advice of stakeholders and empirical data.

In the story above Fiona received two suggestions for improvements, one of which seemed more in keeping with the original product vision than the other. It would have been easy for Fiona to acquiesce—to just do what the stakeholders wanted, wrap up the meeting, and move on. Instead she used the feedback to have a conversation about the product vision, and to build consensus around collecting data about what the teachers were actually experiencing so they could make informed decisions about how to refocus the product to meet changing needs.

Do you tend to accept too much feedback or dismiss feedback too easily?

Listen Well

"We don't see the world as it is, we see it as we are."
Anais Nin

As we explored in "Informed," people have many filters and pre-conceptions that bias what they see and hear. Too often, we see only what we expect to see. Great product owners, therefore, have learned to purposefully avoid developing blind spots by becoming more aware of their own go-to filters and by training themselves to listen beyond their own personal filters so that they can hear valuable feedback when it is offered, even if it is not what they would like to hear. Of course, like Fiona, they will also be sure to filter out any feedback that is not useful, for example, feedback that is incorrect or complicated by ulterior motives.

Listening is a data-gathering skill that can be developed, so great product owners work tirelessly on improving their competency in this area. In his *7 Habits* book, Stephen Covey writes that "most people do not listen with the intent to understand; they listen with the intent to reply" (239). Try to notice when you are simply waiting for someone to stop talking so that you can speak. When you notice this happening, catch yourself and stop, let your thought go and just listen…really listen to what the other person is saying.

Then go further, listen for what they are *not saying*. Then ask them to go further; to expand on what they are saying. Endeavour to understand what is behind the words, what they are feeling, what might be driving them. Put yourself in their position, empathise with them. Practicing this type of listening will not only expand your data-gathering abilities but also help build rapport with your colleagues and stakeholders. People value being heard—it is the easiest, cheapest gift you can give. And while giving, you can learn a lot.

The sprint review, as Fiona demonstrated in the story above, is a wonderfully fertile ground for learning as a product owner, if you are prepared to listen.

Use Data to Point the Way

Let's look at Fiona's actions during the sprint review more closely. The first thing Fiona did was to take stock of her stakeholders and their connection to the users. One stakeholder had not spoken directly to any of the teachers and might not fully understand their actual needs. The other represented a different user entirely—a secondary or perhaps even negative persona for the original product vision (For more on personas, See "Empowering" page 180). Product owners should take into consideration the background and knowledge of their stakeholders when considering their feedback—and weight it accordingly. (See also, Matrix of Influence in Decisive.)

The next thing Fiona did was to re-establish a shared understanding of the goal of the project among the stakeholders, many of whom were new to the project since the vision had been established. She then explained how and why she would like them to invest in gathering data to decide how to evolve that product vision moving forward. The product vision isn't a once-and-done activity. Like most things in agile projects, it evolves over time based on the empirical feedback received during product development.

Like many great product owners, Fiona demonstrated the versatility to evolve the product and also the determination to prioritise data and product vision over emotions and feelings.

Get Powerful, Actionable Feedback

There's a reason the sprint review is not called a sprint demo. Sprint reviews were not meant to be a one-way narrative report of what features have been completed but rather a collaborative, tangible, actionable exploration of what has been delivered and how it will affect the product going forward.

In order for the sprint review to be as valuable as possible, great product owners tend to take the opportunity to ask powerful questions of those attending. Perhaps you could ask the stakeholders present to give a *Net Promotor Score* or to play the *Perfection Game* on what they have seen.

The Net Promoter Score, a concept from Bain & Company, involves stakeholders rating the functionality demonstrated on a scale of 0-10 in terms of how likely they are to recommend the product increment to a friend or relative. That rating is then backed up by an explanation.

The Perfection Game, which I first read about on *The McCarthy Show* website, is similar in that it, too, invites stakeholders to rate what they have seen of a scale of 1-10 but the difference is that the stakeholder's score is based on how much value they believe they can add with their feedback. If they cannot think of any way to make things better, then they would score it a 10. One of the rules of the Perfection Game is that feedback is only invited "in the positive." In other words, people are asked to describe what they currently like and what they could suggest to make it perfect.

Change Course as Needed

Change is hard. Even when a product owner understands that agile projects are all about change, it can still be difficult to fight the natural tendencies of pride and perfectionism to let go of an existing idea or preconceived notion. On the flip side, it can be equally challenging to fight through an innate desire to please people in order to say no to a group of stakeholders, especially when they are also your clients.

The good news is that by remaining versatile, great product owners are able to pivot to new ideas based on feedback and data, to find alternate solutions when a path is blocked, and to lead effectively in the most difficult situations.

DRIVEN

Empowering

"Leaders become great, not because of their power,
but because of their ability to empower others."
John Maxwell

One of the keys to successful agile product management is understanding and mastering the potentially tricky balance of collaboration and autonomy required in an agile environment. The first step in doing so is to reflect on one of the *Principles Behind the Agile Manifesto*, which states that *"business people and developers must work together daily throughout the project."* What exactly does that mean—work together daily? Are product owners expected to remain with the team at all times, just in case they are needed?

No. The reality is there just aren't enough hours in the day to sit with development teams every moment. Furthermore, although a product development effort will likely fail if you spend too little time with the development team, it is just as likely to fail if you spend *too much* time with the development team—it will just fail for different reasons. That's why great product owners work closely with other stakeholders, research the market, plan for releases, gather requirements, and elicit feedback—all without neglecting the development team.

How? By empowering development teams to claim greater autonomy.

The next two stories show how great product owners use agile techniques and artefacts to encourage autonomy while also embracing the regular reflection points at the end of iterations to find the right balance of collaboration and empowerment.

After just a quick glance, Lawrence's heart sank a little.

Lead and Inspire

Good product owners lead from the front.
Great product owners lead from within.

"Ping"

Another email dropped into Lawrence's inbox just as his phone buzzed with a notification of a new text message. After just a quick glance, Lawrence's heart sank a little. Both the email and the text were from members of the development team. Each was asking for his opinion on various changes the team had made to the design.

Lawrence knew that this was how it was supposed to be in an agile team—he'd helped design the *continuous customer collaboration* posters that were currently on display throughout the office. But with questions seemingly every five minutes, he never had time to think. And even though the questions were good ones, he had resorted to hiding in small meeting rooms or tacking on extra days to his site visits so the team couldn't find him.

It was at times like these that he forced himself to remember the bad old days. The days when the meetings with the development team were sporadic and infrequent. Times when the team would go dark for months only to build something that completely missed the point. Lawrence could remember accusing teams of wasting time by indulging in the latest new technology, or of cutting corners to make delivery easier. And he could remember teams blaming him for writing the wrong requirements or including vague or inaccurate specifications.

So, as tiring as it was, the fact that the team were checking with him on a regular basis was an immense improvement. And the fact that he and the team could get feedback from the stakeholders on a tangible delivery every couple of weeks had vastly increased the quality of the products being built.

Yet as three new emails came in, Lawrence realised that he couldn't continue working at this pace. It just wasn't sustainable. And Lawrence was pretty sure there was something to do with sustainable pace in the Agile Manifesto.

He picked up the phone and called Vicky, the team's ScrumMaster. After hearing a brief recap of Lawrence's frustrations, Vicky suggested that they should all talk about it in the upcoming end-of-iteration retrospective.

In the retrospective, Lawrence first made sure the team knew how happy he was with the effects of their increased collaboration: The product quality had increased, and the fact that the team were asking him questions showed they really cared about delivering the right thing, which he greatly appreciated.

He then explained that he was stretched too thin. He suggested that one reason might be that they were asking him too many questions.

He asked them to consider whether there were times when they could just make a decision themselves, and whether perhaps in some situations they might make a better decision than he would have anyway.

Vicky facilitated an open discussion, during which members of the development team admitted that they were afraid of disappointing Lawrence or wasting effort by making the wrong choice. They explained that they also weren't sure when they should ask for Lawrence's decision and when they should make a decision for themselves. They needed help determining where that line should be drawn.

"I can understand all of those concerns," Lawrence admitted. "Especially given our history, where, if you built something I wasn't expecting to see then you were made to feel bad. So how can I help you to be more comfortable in making more decisions yourself?" he asked.

Vicky suggested that the team break up into smaller groups and think of experiments they could run to try to "define the line." After some time, the team came back together to discuss the various options. In the end, Lawrence and the team settled on two options to try.

Firstly, Lawrence agreed to attend the daily scrum (the team's 15-minute morning meeting where they planned what they were going to do that day) so that the team could ask him any clarification questions then. Given the time constraints of that meeting, the team realised they would have to prioritise their questions, but felt that most could be easily and quickly addressed. Vicky also recommended that when a question required a long discussion, research, or a complex answer, Lawrence could address it on a one-on-one basis immediately following the meeting, so as not to overflow the meeting timebox. Everyone suspected that this one change would greatly reduce the email and text questions throughout the day without blocking progress.

Secondly the development team asked Lawrence if they could gather some benchmarks regarding the "line" by creating a flag system. Outside of the daily scrum, whenever a team member asked a question, Lawrence would respond with one of three color-coded answers:

Red: It must be exactly like this.

Amber: It should be something like this. Here are my constraints; solve it as best you can.

Green: It's up to you.

As ScrumMaster, Vicky would capture the data and try to establish patterns or rules of thumb to discuss in the next retrospective.

Both Lawrence and the rest of the team thought these two changes were a good start to bringing the amount of collaboration back into more of a healthy balance.

Find the Right Balance

"Our product owner is never around. If they spent more time with us, then we would be fine."

As I mentioned earlier in the book, product owner availability is probably the number one complaint that I hear from agile teams, which isn't too surprising because the product owner role is so demanding. However, my experience indicates that product owners probably shouldn't be as on-demand as most development teams would like.

The *Principles behind the Agile Manifesto* states, "Business people and developers must work together daily throughout the project." The aim of this principle is to encourage greater collaboration, get feedback earlier and build a relationship. However, if product owners were to spend all day every day with their development teams then they would end up neglecting the other part of their role: collaborating with the stakeholders outside of the team to determine what needs to happen next, to get feedback on what has been built, to prepare for future deployments, and so on.

Would you say you are more at risk of spending too much time with your development team, or too little?

What would the team say?

While spending too little time with the team will inevitably introduce the risk of the development team thrashing with uncertainty or making assumptions that could prove incorrect, spending too much time with the development team can also stifle their independence and creativity. They will find it too easy to ask for an answer, which means the project loses out on the potential for proactive innovation.

Finding the right degree of direct collaboration can take time. For most product owners, working closely with the development team is a new concept, so they must consciously carve out time from their other responsibilities. At first, development teams are usually crying out for more time from their busy product owner, who has many parties competing for his attention. Then, as the product owner sees the benefits of working closely with a development team, the product owner tends to spend too much time with the development team, and soon the other stakeholders are the ones crying out for more time.

In this way, collaboration between a product owner and development team usually swings like a pendulum, from too little to too much, until it finally settles in a comfortable middle. They tend to arrive at this middle ground through a period of trial and error.

Overcome Your Own Fears

Few product owners (or even managers) will admit to it, but one of the biggest obstacles to empowering teams to make their own decisions is the fear that accompanies letting go. For example, many years ago, I was working with a new client and we were talking about the principles of trusting the team. One of the managers said, "You see, Geoff; this is the problem. People are lazy and you can't trust lazy people with important decisions. If you give people autonomy over their own work, then they will just do the bare minimum. People need to be managed."

I admit that I was a bit flustered and taken aback by such a stance. I disagreed with him but I was also certain that he was equally sure that his opinion was valid. While I was thinking of how to respond, one of his colleagues thankfully filled the awkward silence.

"That's interesting," he said. "I haven't had that experience. Are you just hiring badly or what?"

There were a few laughs but then a serious debate ensued about whether most of the people who worked for this manager—and in fact people in general—were inherently lazy and untrustworthy or whether people who appeared lazy were merely reacting to their environment. In the end the general consensus in the room was that, although a few people are in fact untrustworthy, the vast majority are trustworthy unless they are put into an environment where they are perceived to be lazy. This led to a more specific discussion about cynicism between the product owner and the development team—a cynicism that can run both ways.

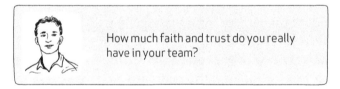

How much faith and trust do you really have in your team?

Development teams often start out with a stereotype of customers who always change their minds or users who don't know what they want. Product owners begin with the belief that developers are all looking to 'geek out' on new technology rather than deliver something useful. We all begin in a place of misconceptions and apprehension. Yet, to quote former American politician Henry Stimson: "The only way to make a man trustworthy is to trust him." So trust we must.

I agree that by trusting someone you risk being proven wrong and taken advantage of but I think that's better than the alternative:

transactional relationships built on cynicism. I'm sure there are many organisations out there with that culture, and many of them may be successful, but they aren't places I would want to work. The good news is that the evolution towards an ideal balance between collaboration and empowerment is a trial and error process. In other words, you don't have to have full trust in the team's decision-making skills today. You just have to have enough trust to let go a little bit—to empower them to make a small decision today. Then, as the relationship with the team improves, begin to move the line further toward empowerment a bit at a time. Yes, you'll eventually go too far and let go of a decision you should have made yourself. But that's OK. It's only one decision and it can be walked back. That is the beauty of iterative development. You build, reflect, and revise based on what you learn. That goes not only for the product but for the relationship with the team as well.

Work *With* the Team

Speaking of relationships, one interesting thing to look out for is how you and the development team view your relationship. Is it a customer-supplier relationship? Or a partnership? There are pros and cons to both, but generally speaking the best product owners work toward being in partnership with the development team.

Here's why: Teams that see you as their customer may not feel comfortable with transparency and may hesitate before making suggestions or even asking questions. They may stand too much on ceremony and avoid taking too many risks. When a team views themselves in a contractual relationship they have a tendency to "protect their position," to ensure their safety should things go wrong.

Listen out for subtle clues in the language the team use that may indicate they view you as a customer rather than a collaborator.

When the team use the word we, does that seem to include you or are you outside of that collective?

Do they talk about delivering things for you or with you?

Great product owners work tirelessly to create a positive, mutually respectful relationship with their teams. As a true partnership develops between the product owner and the team, they waste less energy on relationship preservation, and instead pour all their energy into the product.

Ease Performance Anxiety

One psychological aspect that can stand in the way of this kind of partnership is performance anxiety. Development team members can suffer from this for many reasons, including lack of practice, fear of repercussion, cultural expectations (not expected to question someone more senior or "customer is always right"), or just simply being introverted. Great product owners are aware of signs of performance anxiety in others and work to alleviate that fear.

People who suffer from performance anxiety may avoid conversations or reduce the bandwidth (phone call instead of face to face;

email instead of phone call). They might resist asking for feedback until it is too late to take action. They often hesitate to ask for help or to engage in collaborative meetings such as the daily scrum or retrospectives. All of these avoidance tactics impact how effective the team will be, and ultimately the quality and speed of delivery.

One of the best ways to help others overcome performance anxiety in their interactions with you is to increase psychological safety through empathy and understanding. For example, in the story, after the team had bravely and transparently expressed some of the reasons why they felt uncomfortable making decisions, Lawrence responded by saying, "I can understand all of those concerns … Especially given our history, where, if you built something I wasn't expecting to see then you were made to feel bad. So how can I help you to be more comfortable in making more decisions yourself?"

Another excellent way to mitigate performance anxiety is to model the behaviours that you are hoping to encourage in others. If you want people to be vulnerable, be vulnerable yourself. Also, when the team do push themselves and make themselves vulnerable, perhaps by telling you something they fear you may not want to hear, be sure to act in a way that won't discourage them from being open with you again in the future. Thank them for their honesty and their courage and explain how useful that information is to you.

As the team assume more autonomy they will inevitably make some mistakes or misconstrue requirements. It is important not to over-react to these setbacks; doing so is sure to force the team back into their shell. Instead, as difficult as it may be, welcome this as part of the team's growth and treat it as an opportunity to discuss your real needs and improve your communication and collaborative process to avoid future misinterpretations.

Schedule Time for Direct Collaboration

I've talked at length about a few of the psychological impediments to balancing collaboration and empowerment, including the fear that can accompany letting go, the need to partner with the development team, and the team's anxiety about making a wrong choice. Let's return now to the story and discuss the practical steps Lawrence and the team took to find a more healthy degree of collaboration.

The first change they made was for Lawrence to attend the daily scrum whenever possible so that he could answer everyone's questions at one time. Setting aside certain days or times during the week where you are available to answer questions and brainstorm solutions is often a great start toward interacting regularly with the team. Many product owners attend the daily scrums and many also hold a weekly backlog refinement workshop to go through a few user stories for an hour or two.

Another way to create balance is to consider only attending the first half of the team's sprint planning sessions. In Scrum, this would equate to Sprint Planning Meeting Part One, where the team are attempting to work out *what* they think they are capable of achieving this sprint. When the team move on to the second half – working out *how* they plan to achieve that plan, try stepping out. Remain nearby or available via phone should the team need you, but leave the team some space to determine how they will achieve the work you have described.

> Could you add value to the team's daily scrum meetings?
>
> Are you currently reducing the value they get from these meetings?

Create Benchmarks

The second change Lawrence and the team made was to educate themselves about the kinds of decisions the team might be able to make on their own. They created a color-coded benchmark system to help gather data and agreed to discuss it at a future retrospective.

Taking an iteration or two to capture some real data can help the team determine when they should ask for clarification. As you receive questions, flag whether this is an instance where you need to make the decision or whether it's something you could leave to the team. The key here is to capture this data and then reflect on it so the team, and you, can draw some initial conclusions. The goal is to help the team develop more autonomy within the agreed-upon framework, with the understanding that you'll continuously be fine-tuning where the "line" is.

Hire Well and Invest in People

A third practical step that you can make is to look closely at your team-building practices and job descriptions. Managers and great product owners in an agile-minded organisation focus on hiring and/ or building teams of proactive, collaborative, entrepreneurial people. It's much easier to trust people who demonstrate these attributes.

The hard truth is that if you hire the wrong people—or you inherit a team that you don't know very well—it's much harder to take a leap of faith toward trusting those people to make good decisions. The good news, as I alluded to earlier, is that because Scrum and agile use such short iterations, you don't have to wait long to see if trusting the team has paid off. I remember Ken Schwaber (the co-creator of Scrum) joking once that:

"Scrum even works with idiots. You can get a bunch of people who have never done software development, have never been to college—who hate each other—and put them in a room for 30 days with a prioritised product backlog; and Scrum would work fine. It will work fine because in 30 days you will know empirically what that team is capable of and then you can choose what to do with that information about the team."

Ken intended this as hyperbole—you'd never intentionally build such a team, but he said it because there is an element of truth in there. If the team you have is terribly incompetent, or untrustworthy, then you will know after just one iteration. And then you can choose to act on that knowledge.

- Perhaps you sack them and stop the project.
- Perhaps you work on the environment that is encouraging undesirable behaviours.
- Perhaps you invest in the team's development.

This reminds me of another joke where the CFO of a company says, "What happens if we invest in the training and development of our people and then they just leave?" To which the CIO replies, "What if we don't invest in their training and development and they *stay*?!"

To the extent that you are able to influence hiring and employee development practices, move purposefully toward hiring and developing people who are worthy of trust and who can act with autonomy.

Don't Delegate Everything

As product owners empower the team to make some decisions themselves, they run another risk—one of losing some of their own autonomy. Similarly, as product owners solicit feedback from other stakeholders, it can be difficult to remain firm on certain issues. As with everything else surrounding collaboration, balance is the key.

If the balance has tipped too much towards a customer-supplier relationship, perhaps look back to "Informed" and work on developing greater rapport with the team. If, on the other hand, you feel that you have given away too much of your own autonomy, use the retrospectives to discuss this concern with the team.

Remember that product owners are empowered to make the final decision. The idea here is not to delegate all authority to the development team so that you can keep your inbox clear of questions! Instead, it is to find ways to reduce the burden of decision making by concentrating decisions into certain time blocks and by helping the team understand which decisions they should make themselves.

Have you explicitly discussed what you are comfortable delegating to the team and what you will retain authority over?

Don't Forget to Empower Yourself

So far the focus has been on empowering the development team because, in most organisations, the development team needs significant support, encouragement and trust to join in the product development process in a more equal manner. However, product owners can also struggle with being empowered themselves. I've encountered many product owners who lack the environment, support, trust and authority they need to move the product forward.

If you frequently need to justify your decisions or can't make decisions in a timely manner because you don't have the authority you need to do so, you might need to engage your own leadership in a conversation about trust. Then, use the agile development process to help address the concerns that come to light.

First, remind senior leadership that with short iterations, they'll see the results of your decisions quickly. You and they can then use the feedback from each iteration to make any necessary adjustments. You might be able to further lessen their fears by addressing any specific concerns that they might raise. For example, if people are hesitant to trust you because they worry that you lack experience or have questionable judgement, then you might be able to ameliorate those concerns by increasing the experience level of your product owner team and demonstrating the collaborative decision-making process you undertake with that team.

If people believe that the product you are building is too risky or the market you are building for is too volatile or too unknown, you can show them how you are prioritising to minimise risk or gain learning fast.

An empowered product owner collaborating iteratively and incrementally with an empowered development team is a hallmark of a great product development process. Great product owners strive to increase their own autonomy so that they have the authority to make timely decisions while simultaneously expanding the autonomy of the development team so that they aren't buried under the weight of *too many* decisions. Great product owners also know that empowering teams to make decisions often results in much more creative solutions—a benefit that's too important to ignore.

How many people's approval do you need when you have decided what needs to be done?

What is the risk of your decision being over-ruled or overturned?

"Gavin's a real family guy. He didn't have a great time as a child, his parents broke up and so he doesn't have many good memories of when he was small."

Show and Tell

Good product owners write good stories.
Great product owners tell great stories.

A collaborative balance between the team and product owner is only one way to empower the team. Another practice great product owners follow is to give teams the context for creativity. To understand what this means, let's return to the characters from the earlier story (Lawrence, Vicky, and the development team). We join them later in the project during the planning session for Sprint 7.

Vicky, the ScrumMaster, picked up the next card off the wall and read it aloud.

Figure E-1: The user story card Vicky picked off the wall

She gestured to the development team, who were all sitting around a table, and asked, "What do you think guys? Anything you need to know about this one before you can estimate it?"

One of the team members, Rachel, asked a few questions about whether the photo storage was automatic or manual and whether there needed to be an option for subfolders and naming the files. Another team member, Steve, asked what the rules needed to be for deleting the files. These questions were all aimed at helping the team get a feel for the scope of the story and Lawrence, as product owner, did his best to answer them while Vicky added a few details to the card.

The sprint planning session was progressing but, from Lawrence's point of view, it felt a bit painful and forced, like the team were going through the motions, with little or no energy or enthusiasm.

"What's the matter, guys?" Lawrence asked. He then explained his concerns about the energy levels.

"Nothing's the matter, but I see your point about our lack of energy," Rachel replied. "Perhaps it would help if you could tell us a bit more about how you see the Gavin persona using this feature."

Lawrence grasped this opportunity, stood up, walked to the whiteboard at the front of the room and proceeded to tell the team all about Gavin, the fictional user persona he had created to represent the product's target demographic.

"Gavin's a real family guy. He didn't have a great time as a child, his parents broke up and so he doesn't have many good memories of when he was small. In fact, his memory isn't great in general and so he really wants to capture all the happy times he has had and will have with his new family. He and his wife have just had twins you see – the sleep deprivation isn't helping with the memory issue – and this, coupled with his skepticism about the reliability of technology means that he really wants to feel comfortable that all the photos he takes are backed up and will never get lost. He struggles with setting things up so he needs it to be easy and he wants one place where his photos and his wife's photos are stored."

Everyone knew Gavin was only a persona but Lawrence began talking so passionately about Gavin's situation and how he would use this feature that the team could almost believe he was real.

"Wow," said Rachel. "That helped a lot! In fact, I had presumed that because you had mentioned the cloud that Gavin was quite proficient with technology but now I can see it's not quite like that. I can also see why the family account and some of the other features are relevant now."

Rachel then stood up and walked to the whiteboard to sketch out how she saw the feature taking place and linking to another part of the system. This then encouraged Steve to get up and, before long, story cards were being torn up, rewritten, stuck on the walls, and linked to one another. The planning session developed an energy that none of the team had ever seen before, all from a little storytelling.

Take Advantage of User Stories

One of the biggest causes of friction between a product manager and a development team is in the interpretation of requirements. Development teams often complain of vague, ambiguous requirements while product managers often complain that development teams just don't get it and make terrible assumptions. All of the psychological factors we discussed earlier—fear of letting go, performance anxiety, and a lack of a true partnership—all come into play again.

As a result, requirements documentation tends to become bloated, as people attempt to capture every possible interpretation, and in many cases adopt the language of a legal contract to avoid ambiguity or, just as likely, protect themselves against blame when the inevitable disagreements happen.

The *user story* was born as an antidote to this problem. A user story came from eXtreme Programming (XP)—one of the forerunners in the agile software development movement. As shown in the story about Lawrence and the team, a user story is a unit of scope for a project written in a particular format, usually transcribed onto a portable and tangible artefact, such as an index card, and intended to be a token used in conversation between the product owner and the team. Like requirements, user stories are written by product owners, but they avoid many of the problems of bloated requirements documents by leaving the specific details for a future conversation.

When it was first introduced, the user story was a radically new way of formatting requirements, but it quickly became the standard way of writing requirements on agile projects. By positioning requirements in the context of the user and, most importantly, framing the reason for that user's need, much greater empathy was developed between developer and customer, which in turn led to better solutions.

 How well are your requirements helping the team empathise with the product's users?

Create Compelling Personas

Another great way for product owners to understand who to build their products for is to create some personas. Personas are representations of potential, actual, or even fictional users or consumers of our product. In the story, Lawrence had written a user story about Gavin, a persona he had developed to relay certain information about the product's users.

Personas come from the field of user experience. I first came across the concept in Alan Cooper's 2004 book *The Inmates Are Running the Asylum: Why High-tech Products Drive Us Crazy and How to Restore the Sanity.* Personas are an attempt to turn market research into tangible examples of a specific user or user group that the product is to be developed for.

While there is no standard structure or presentation format for a persona, they commonly contain information such as:

- The user's goals from using the product
- The user's expectations, demands, and needs of the product
- An idea of how this user would likely interact with the product
- A description of who this person is, how they think, and what they value
- Examples of things they might typically say, think, or do
- Pictures of the user in action

Personas can be an incredibly useful tool for product owners as they look to focus on the most important demographics and guide the development of the product toward solving real people's goals. They are a constant reminder of why the product is being developed and how it will ultimately be judged.

Personas are also useful for the development team in helping them make good decisions during development in order to optimise design. Many development teams that I have worked with cite how much of a motivational difference it makes to have a picture of actual users rather than just focus on building a product. The product owners of these same teams also cite how much more innovative and intuitive the solutions are that these teams come up with. I don't think that is a coincidence.

On most projects, there will be more than one type of valuable persona, so product owners and teams should develop as many as seem appropriate. For example, all teams can identify at least one *primary persona* - an individual representing the main demographic for your product. This persona will drive the design; the product ultimately should match their goals. Many products also have *secondary persona* whose needs will be met if possible but, when push comes to shove, will be prioritised below the needs of the primary persona.

Many product owners find it useful to think of the *negative personas* or *exclusionary personas*. These are people who definitely are *not* the intended audience for the product. For example, a computer hacker is a negative persona for a software product. Other negative personas include someone who doesn't have the disposable income required to buy the product or perhaps someone who will never buy the product because of brand loyalty to a competitor. Defining negative personas can help ensure that companies avoid wasting money marketing to the wrong people or allowing the wrong audience's design considerations to enter into the product development effort. It can also help block any malicious actions.

How well do you understand who will be using your product and how they will be using – or mis-using it?

Below is an example of what a persona might look like for a travel website

Figure E-2. Personas help tell the story of a product's users.

Tell the Users' Stories

But the writing of the persona or user story is just one part of the story (excuse the pun). I've yet to hear a child say, "Daddy, will you *write* me a story…PLEEEASE?" People want to *hear* stories so that they can become part of them.

User stories were never intended to be a tool for capturing requirements so efficiently that they could be implemented without collaboration. On the contrary, they were intended to provoke conversation and facilitate collaborative problem solving. Therefore, the best user stories don't prescribe a solution but rather frame a problem to be solved. Product owners don't write the entire story on the card but instead invite the team to collaboratively evolve the story. In effect, the conversations around user stories empower the team to find creative solutions.

In the story, Lawrence and the team felt that the planning session lacked the creative energy necessary to produce a truly exceptional product. Just as Lawrence stood up and told the real story of Gavin (where he is coming from, what he is trying to achieve, what his frustrations are, what his hopes are), the best product owners *tell* the stories of their users—to make the users' needs resonate with the product development team. In doing so, they help establish emotional connections and empathy between the people who are building the product and the people they are building the product for. I have seen dramatic effects of moving from writing to telling time and time again.

In his book *Improv-ing Agile Teams – Using Constraints to Unlock Creativity*, Paul Goddard explains how improvisational theatre actors follow some key elements of storytelling that agile teams (and product owners) can benefit from:

1. They keep it simple. They don't try and over-complicate the storyline. The main thrust of the story should be easily summed up in one or two sentences.

2. They reincorporate the past. They ensure continuity and congruence by connecting the present and the future with what has gone before.

3. They relate to the characters. Improv actors find ways to help the audience empathise and connect with the characters in the story they are telling. Similarly, great product owners allow the development team to empathise and connect with those who will use or consume what the team are going to build. They allow the team to see how the new feature will impact the character and how their life will be changed.

4. They finish the story. Storytellers allow the audience to achieve closure. Similarly, product owners should help teams know when they are done. Usually this involves providing objective conditions of satisfaction or acceptance criteria to the user story but it can also include something more personal and subjective, such as a description of the state of mind or newfound ability of the character. In keeping with the theme of giving a problem rather than a solution, great storytellers and product owners often define the ending before the middle of the story. They allow the team to work out and evolve how they get from the start to the end.

> What element of the user's world do you know least about?
>
> How could you increase your knowledge about this area?

Acknowledge the Fear

Let's be honest. Telling stories can be intimidating if not downright scary. Any performance anxiety you have lurking in your psyche can come roaring to life as you consider how others might react if you make a mistake or if the story doesn't resonate and they look at you oddly.

The first step in moving through the fear is to realise it is normal. In my experience, and according to *statisticbrain.com*, 75%+ of people have a fear of "performing" in public. I have observed that a great deal of this anxiety is down to the human tendency to "catastrophize" and (over) think about future consequences. The best antidote I've found to this is to practice mindfulness. Stay in the moment and rationally analyse the assumptions you are making about the consequences and likelihood of "failing".

Recognize, too, that your mindset and motivational strategy might be a factor in your anxiety. When we are pessimistic or cynical, there is a good chance we will think the worst is going to happen and unconsciously adopt an *away from* motivational strategy. When this happens we typically adopt behaviours that are very defensive and risk averse in order to protect ourselves from a bad outcome. Awareness gives us choice. When we are more self-aware, we can choose to adopt a more helpful motivational strategy. Also, because what we choose to focus on has a large impact on what is likely to happen, adopting a *towards* strategy is a great way of tackling both cynicism and performance anxiety. Instead of focusing on what might go wrong, instead tell yourself what positive outcomes there could be as a result of your "performance," not just in terms of the specific outcome, but in other ways as well; for example, self-development, self-confidence and modelling the behaviour to others.

Story Structure

After you've worked up the courage to tell a story, remember that following a structure can help make telling a story much less intimidating. Although there is no single correct structure for a story, the following techniques might be helpful as you begin telling the stories of your users.

A **dramatic arc** begins with an introduction, where you set the scene and introduce the characters and the context. Then, at some point, you name a complication or a twist: a challenge that one or all of the characters face in the story. From this point on, the bulk of the story, the middle, focuses on overcoming the complication and any other related challenges that surface. This leads to a climax where the main problem is solved or the initial challenge is overcome. Finally, there is the wrap-up, or denouement, where all the loose ends are tied up and the audience receive closure. Some arcs also include a coda, where the moral of the story is revealed or highlighted. Figure E-2 shows a typical dramatic arc.

Standard Story Structure

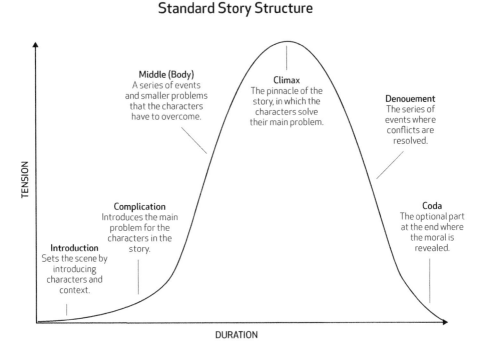

Figure E-3. Many stories follow a similar dramatic arc.

Story Spines

Story spines is an exercise that allows you to practice telling stories one sentence or paragraph at a time to lay out the rough journey for the audience. Begin by completing the following sentences:

> Once upon a time…(introduce the character)
> And every day…(introduce their current situation)
> But, one day…(the character's situation changes somehow)
> And because of that…(there is an impact to the character)

And because of that…(perhaps there is a knock-on effect or escalation)
Until finally…(something happens to address the change introduced in the story)
And ever since then…(the character either succeeds or fails in their efforts)

Once the rough story has been told, you can fill in the details with the team as necessary. If you are feeling adventurous, a fun variation of this is to complete the same story structure but in a non-linear order. So, for example, you could perhaps complete the sentences in the following order instead:

Once upon a time…(introduce the character)
And ever since then…(the character either succeeds or fails in their efforts)
And every day…(introduce their current situation)
But, one day…(the character's situation changes somehow)
Until finally…(something happens to address the change introduced in the story)
And because of that…(there is an impact to the character)
And because of that…(perhaps there is a knock-on effect or escalation)

This is also an exercise that you can run in groups or teams where each person takes a sentence to complete one at a time and, as a group, evolve the story.

User Poems

If storytelling isn't your cup of tea, try speaking in rhyme. One of the most creative and enjoyable examples of expanding on the traditional user story format that I have come across is the user poem and, in particular, the user limerick. If you are unfamiliar with limericks, just know that each limerick is five lines long, with lines 1, 2 and 5 rhyming with each other and lines 3 and 4 rhyming with each other. Lines 3 and 4 have fewer syllables than lines 1, 2 and 5. For example:

A team from the town Balamory
Grew tired of the old user story
Though it seemed a bit strange
They used poems for a change
Which led them to rhythmical glory.

Note that the rhymes don't have to be precise to be effective. If we were to apply this approach to the user story Lawrence had written, we might come up with something like:

A tool to preserve precious memories
Is where we should put all our energies
For Gavin, the new Dad
Fear of losing his iPad
Is one of his life's biggest enemies.

I have generally been pleasantly surprised by how quickly product owners get into the spirit of user poems and enjoy the challenge of writing some to speak aloud. However, the biggest barrier is self-consciousness so give yourself some slack. As you begin to leave your comfort zone, don't push yourself too far too quickly.

The area just outside of our comfort zone is often referred to as the stretch zone. In the stretch zone we experience some degree of discomfort but this is the area where learning and growth is most likely to occur and where confidence may grow.

If we stretch too much or too soon, however, then we can end up in the panic zone, where we are unlikely to be capable of learning or growth.

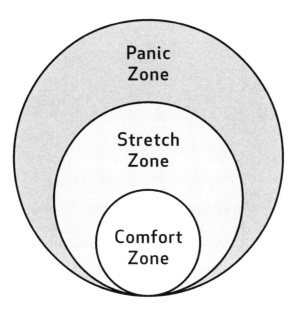

Figure E-4. Venture into the stretch zone for growth.

The point of this is not for you to become the next poet laureate but rather to experiment with different ways of getting user needs across and engaging your team.

A story conveys user needs
If well written the team often succeeds
Don't focus on spelling
The value's in the telling
So think hard about how well it reads

If you aren't keen on limericks, then experiment with different forms of poetry such as the haiku, the dirge, the ballad, the sonnet, the stanza, the couplet or the quatrain; or simply go for some free-form verse.

What might be the benefits of pushing yourself out of your comfort zone?

For you? For the team? For the product?

I just want to re-emphasise though the idea is not to get everyone writing limericks but rather to re-ignite the engagement between the team and the work. The power is not in the writing but the telling:

If the poetry's getting you vexed
Then just stick to the plain old straight text
The point's not the rhyming
Or even the timing
But getting across the context

Conclusion

All product development efforts are effectively stories; you and the product development team are characters in that story. There is a problem to solve and a journey that you will all go through in attempting to solve that problem together.

Good product owners empower their teams to get involved in the problem-solving process; they don't prescribe arbitrary solutions but rather invite teams to engage with them. Great product owners provide structure and context through tools such as user stories and personas, and unleash the creativity and curiosity of the team through the power of storytelling – both their own and the team's.

The best stories are ones that are created together, where nobody can really tell whose story it was when they look back at it. Product owners are responsible for identifying the problems that need solving for their users but *how* they get solved is not necessarily their responsibility. Great product owners harness the collective intelligence, creativity and experience of their teams to create truly compelling results.

DRIVEN

Negotiable

"Dream in a pragmatic way."
Aldous Huxley

There will forever be two conflicting forces acting upon a product owner: the desire for perfection and the need to deliver a high-quality product on time and on budget. DRIVEN product owners want to build the best product possible. To do this, they must be prepared to push the boundaries, challenge themselves and those around them, and to question their assumptions about what is possible.

Simultaneously, though, good product owners know that chasing perfection at the expense of bringing the product to market is a sure way to fail. After all, if the definition of "good enough" is too big to achieve, then either the product will be released with compromised integrity and quality or the product will linger in an endless development loop, never being deemed worthy of release.

Great product owners, therefore, have learned how to **negotiate** a balance between the dream of a perfect product and the practical need to release a high-quality product into the market in a timely and cost-effective manner. Negotiation doesn't necessarily mean compromising or gaining consensus. As we saw earlier, in "Decisive", product owners must be prepared to make the tough calls; they can't afford to please everyone if it means the product will suffer. That is why great product owners strive for excellence, rather than perfection. And why they find ways to reconcile the needs of many stakeholders in the interest of the overall quality of the product.

Karen could feel one of her migraines coming on.

Appease and Delight

Good product owners represent many different parties.
Great product owners know they can't please everyone.

Karen could feel one of her migraines coming on. The group gathered in the conference room were getting nowhere. It was just getting noisier. She was beginning to regret inviting so many stakeholders to this meeting. Tasked with developing a new face-care product, Karen had sought the input and experience of various people who represented different demographics and different regions. She had also commissioned market research into what consumers were looking for, but the data was not overwhelming in one direction or another.

Steve, head of AsiaPac, was making a very strong case for designing the product for his target market. Yet Carla, the head of the European market, had a very different set of product needs for her target market. To Karen, the differences seemed insurmountable. Just when she was about to call a break for her own wellbeing, Jamie, the Head of Marketing, spoke up. As he did, Karen realised that unlike the others in the room, Jamie had been actually been quiet for a long time.

"OK," Jamie said. "It sounds like everyone has completely valid arguments and the data could be used to justify each of your different ideas. I'm wondering whether we can actually do something radical here that might manage to solve all of our problems."

Karen perked up. She had worked with Jamie for years and knew how creative he could be. If anybody could bring this dysfunctional group of mavericks together, she thought, it would be him.

Jamie continued: "What if we develop a product that we market to both young men and also young women? We can tailor the preferred packaging from the AsiaPac market slightly so it's a little closer to the European preferences. And since most of the recommended scents are from the same general family of fragrances, we'll go with the generic "citrus" as opposed to something more specific such as orange or pomegranate. The product could probably be exfoliating, cleansing, **and** moisturising, which covers the number one preferences from South America, Europe and AsiaPac..." Jamie went on, expertly pulling together almost every requested requirement into one mega product.

When he had finished, he gave Karen a wink and a smile, then sat back in his chair, clearly pleased with the product he had described.

The rest of the room grew suddenly silent as everyone considered Jamie's proposal; Karen could hear herself think for the first time in about an hour. She looked around the room and saw Steve leaning back in his chair, looking at the ceiling, while Carla had her head bent over with her fingers on her temples—her classic "I'm thinking about how I want to react" pose. Eventually, Karen heard mutterings and grumbles of consent from all the participants. They had each had their concerns and requests listened to and seen them taken into account in the new product idea.

Jamie spoke up," What do you think Karen? It seems as though we have a solution we can all agree on."

Karen began to nod but then hesitated. She should have been thrilled, yet something didn't feel right. Maybe it was the fact that she just wasn't used to everyone being in agreement - this bunch of cats had never been so neatly herded before - that discomfited her. Or perhaps it was that she suspected Jamie's solution was less about designing the best product for the market and more about pleasing everyone in the room.

"I think that was an excellent summary, Jamie. I want to thank you and everyone else for all of your input into this discussion and for being willing to compromise in the spirit of agreeing on a product that we could all support…"

She swallowed hard before continuing:

"But something's not quite right here. I don't think you guys are supposed to agree. I don't think there *is* one product that will make all of you, and all of the people you represent, happy. I think if we end up building this compromise version of the product, everyone will be 40 percent happy and nobody will be 90 percent happy."

She paused again.

"I don't want to be the product manager of a camel." Karen said.

The others in the room looked a little puzzled by this comment so she explained.

"There's a quote by Alec Issigonis about how the camel is a horse designed by committee. What it means is that by trying to please everyone, you only end up with something that pleases no one, including our customers. While I appreciate Jamie's solution, I think the best course of action is for me to be ruthless and start with one excellent product—with a plan to develop multiple excellent products over time—as opposed to settling for one less-than-optimal mega-product."

Karen then led the team in defining the separate products that were indirectly being pitched in the room and capturing their characteristics on separate flipcharts. Jamie was tasked with identifying the true common ground between the competing product ideas. One of the factors Karen used to prioritise the rival product designs (along with potential market size, disposable income of target demographic, and other bottom-line factors) was the amount to which each product could potentially cross demographic and geographical boundaries with minimal refactoring in the future. Though this path was initially more difficult than the one Jamie had proposed, Karen felt sure it was the right one to take.

What personal values could you leverage here?

What is important to you that you don't want to compromise?

Stand Up for the Product

Product Owners are faced with an interesting challenge when it comes to negotiations. On the one hand they know that they need to focus on customer and user satisfaction in order for their product or service to be a success. This involves empathising with their stakeholders, listening to them, identifying their problems, and creating solutions for them. Yet they also know that not all users will want the same things and so whatever decision they make will likely be displeasing to one or more user groups. Although they could avoid confrontation by settling for a compromise solution, great product owners choose the more demanding path: excellence through true negotiation.

If you are honest with yourself, how often do you take the difficult yet correct course of action?

What do you think of others that do that?

In the story, Karen was tempted to take the compromise that Jamie had carefully crafted. It would have appeased the most people and put an end to all of the bickering and conflict. Yet Karen also knew deep down that the compromise would not result in the best product. She remembered that ultimately her job is to create an excellent product—her job is not to please the most stakeholders.

Deliberately choosing a solution that will disappoint some users is especially challenging for chronic people pleasers, those who put others' needs before their own and avoid anything that might resemble conflict for fear of someone getting upset. In the story, Karen had to say no, not only to the stakeholders, but also to Jamie, who had clearly worked diligently to arrive at a compromise solution. That isn't always an easy thing to do.

Is there a difference between what your head says is right and what your heart says is right?

Have you considered both?

In my book *The Coach's Casebook*, I address several ways to bring these kinds of people-pleasing tendencies into balance. For example, when faced with a situation where you know you need to choose a course of action that might disappoint people, the first step to minimising any accompanying anxiety is to assess the perceived consequences.

Ask yourself the following questions:

- What do you think will happen if you say no?
- How realistic are those consequences when you think about them objectively?
- If those consequences do manifest, is your decision to say no the real cause?

Answering these questions often makes it easier to make the right decision.

Play Consensus-Building Games

Negotiating with different stakeholders is an essential part of the product owner's job. Few are successful by ignoring or upsetting stakeholders, but attempting to please everyone is also likely to end in failure. As well as being aware of and attempting to manage the tendency to want to please others and avoid conflict, it helps to have some practical product ownership techniques. Techniques such as "pass the cards" and "priority markets" can help you negotiate more effectively with stakeholders. Let's look closely at each of these.

One way to negotiate ideas amongst a group of stakeholders is to use the technique **pass the cards**. This technique is sometimes called *35* or *49* because of the point scoring system used but, for simplicity, and in deference to its name in Jean Tabaka's *Collaboration Explained*, I call it *pass the cards*. Pass the cards can be used to prioritise any set of competing items, such as requirements, features, or even personas. It can even be used to decide which ideas or topics will be discussed further and which actions to take. In this situation we will assume that there are many possible features that could be included into the product and we need to choose only the most important.

This technique requires an even number of people (at least 8), some blank index cards, and enough pens for everyone involved. The steps are as follows:

1. Write each potential feature onto a separate index card.
2. Give each person one of these cards and a pen.
3. Ask everyone to pair up and discuss the two cards that, between them, they are holding.
4. Once they have discussed the two features briefly, ask them to allocate 9 priority points across the two cards based on the

relative value of these features. For example if card 1 is more valuable than card 2 then card 1 would be allocated a higher proportion of the 9 points available. For example, the pair might assign 7 points to card 1 and 2 points to card 2.

5. Ask each pair to write the chosen number of priority points on the back of each card.

6. Ask everyone to swap cards with the person they were just talking to so that everyone is now holding a different card to the one they started the exercise with. This is very important.

7. Begin round 2. During this round, everyone returns to step 3 by pairing up with someone different and comparing two cards.

8. Run this exercise for at least 7 rounds then total up the scores on the backs of each card and lay them out for discussion, with the lowest value items on the left and the highest value items on the right. Begin with the highest value items and work your way down.

9. Now that we have a set of benchmarks, it becomes a lot easier to slot the remaining features into the scale of values that we have established without the necessity of going through this process again. We hear things like "this one is a lot like this one" or "this one is higher than this one but lower than this one". Of course the option remains to run another exercise with the remaining cards should you find it valuable or enjoyable to do so.

Pass the cards is a simple yet engaging and collaborative exercise that allows for everyone's input relatively quickly while avoiding many pitched arguments for people's entrenched positions. Rather than just reiterate how important their idea is, each stakeholder literally has to give their idea away and see what other people think.

Additionally, a number of smaller discussions are a lot easier and quicker than one big discussion and should very quickly provide a representative picture of the opinions of those in the room. One of the jobs of the product owner is to start - and facilitate - discussions about any large discrepancies they may see.

Whose help could you enlist to make negotiating a solution easier?

Another negotiation technique that I have used in many environments is called **Priority Markets** or **Free Market Prioritisation**. This is a technique that Jason Haines and I developed and wrote about when we were both helping an investment bank adopt Scrum.

In this market-based approach, each stakeholder is given some virtual money in the form of development dollars, which they can use to bid on backlog items. The method is fair and democratic in that all stakeholders get a voice in the prioritisation process. It is also open, in that all participants can see how each backlog item was prioritised. The method is also relatively efficient to administer and scales well to large numbers of stakeholders and arbitrarily long lists of backlog items.

Step 0: Set up

We'll assume that the project already has a backlog of development items. For our example we have six backlog items with differing development costs.

The first step is for the product owner to identify the different stakeholders who will be involved in setting the development priorities. The PO should then assign each stakeholder a relative weighting based on their importance to the project.

For the sake of simplicity, we will assume four stakeholders (John, Paul, George and Ringo) with an equal weighting of 1.0 each. (Later in this chapter, I discuss how to handle stakeholders with unequal weightings.)

Now we introduce the concept of development dollars. Development dollars will be used by the stakeholders to bid for and buy changes in the system.

We first create a "bank" of unallocated development dollars. To start the process, we inject an initial number of development dollars into the system. The exact number is not critical and you can tune and adjust this with practice; perhaps start with $10 each to begin with.

At the start we then have a table as shown in Figure N-1:

	STAKEHOLDER			
	John (1.0)	Paul (1.0)	George (1.0)	Ringo (1.0)
Change A				
Change B				
Change C				
Change D				
Change E				
Change F				

Figure N-1. Six backlog items and four stakeholders of equal weight.

Step 1: Dollar Distribution

Now we distribute the unallocated development dollars to the stakeholders based on their weights. After the distribution, each stakeholder has a number of unspent development dollars.

Unallocated	$40

	STAKEHOLDER			
	John (1.0)	Paul (1.0)	George (1.0)	Ringo (1.0)
Change A				
Change B				
Change C				
Change D				
Change E				
Change F				
Unspent	$0	$0	$0	$0

Figure N-2. Start with a certain number of unallocated dollars ($40).

Unallocated	$0

	STAKEHOLDER			
	John (1.0)	Paul (1.0)	George (1.0)	Ringo (1.0)
Change A				
Change B				
Change C				
Change D				
Change E				
Change F				
Unspent	$10	$10	$10	$10

Figure N-3. Divide the unallocated dollars among stakeholders according to weight ($10/each).

Step 2: Bidding

The stakeholders now bid their development dollars on the backlog items in accordance with their preferences. Development dollars that have been bid are deducted from their unspent dollars. Imagine the stakeholders allocate their dollars as follows:

| Unallocated | $0 | | | |

	STAKEHOLDER			
	John (1.0)	Paul (1.0)	George (1.0)	Ringo (1.0)
Change A				
Change B	$3		$2	
Change C		$7	$2	$2
Change D	$4	$1	$4	
Change E	$3	$2	$2	$1
Change F				$7
Unspent	$0	$0	$0	$0

Figure N-4. Each stakeholder bids on the Product Backlog Items (PBIs) that have the highest priority for him or her.

Step 3: Priority Calculation

We next determine the relative value of each item by calculating the total bid of development dollars allocated to it. The developers can then estimate the development cost of each backlog item that has a bid. From there we can calculate the return on investment (ROI) of each backlog item by dividing the total bid by the development cost. Ordering the backlog by largest to smallest ROI gives us our priorities:

Unallocated	$0

	STAKEHOLDER				Total bid	Dev cost	ROI
	John (1.0)	Paul (1.0)	Georg (1.0)	Ringo (1.0)			
Change F				$7	$7	2	3.5
Change D	$4	$1	$4		$9	4	2.3
Change B	$3		$2		$5	3	1.7
Change C		$7	$2	$2	$11	7	1.6
Change E	$3	$2	$2	$1	$8	5	1.6
Change A							
Unspent	$0	$0	$0	$0			

Figure N-5. Use the total bid and development cost to determine the ROI for each PBI. Priortise based on ROI.

Some notes to make on the priorities:

- Ordering by ROI tells us to deliver items in terms of best "bang for the buck". Although *Change C* has the largest total bid, it also has a large development cost and so is further down the priority list.

- *Change F* is at the top of the priorities even though it is important to only a single stakeholder. Given that Ringo allocated $7 to it, *Change F* is clearly critical to him.

- *Change A* has had no development dollars bid against it and is thus at the bottom of the list. In a typical project there will be a large number of items that have no dollars bid against them. This is actually an advantage of the method, as the stakeholders can concentrate their attention on a limited number of critical items on the Product Backlog. Also note that it is not critical to have a development cost estimate at this time for any items that received no bids.

Step 4: Develop for an Iteration

The prioritised backlog is then taken by the developers so they can schedule work for an iteration. If, for example, the developers have the development capacity to complete the first two items - Change F and Change D - in the next iteration, then these changes are then implemented.

Step 5: Reallocation of Dollars

Change F and Change D have been completed and can be archived. The dollars spent on them are now reallocated. The two backlog items had a total of $7 + $9 = $16 spent on them. This amount is first put into the unallocated pot. The completed features (F and D) are removed from the bidding table.

Unallocated	$16

	STAKEHOLDER				Total bid	Dev cost	ROI
	John (1.0)	Paul (1.0)	Georg (1.0)	Ringo (1.0)			
Change B	$3		$2		$5	3	1.7
Change C		$7	$2	$2	$11	7	1.6
Change E	$3	$2	$2	$1	$8	5	1.6
Change A					$0	2	0.0
Unspent	$0	$0	$0	$0			

Figure N-6. Completed features F & D are removed from the table. The dollars allocated to them are put back in the unallocated bin.

For the next round of prioritisation, we then reallocate these dollars among all the stakeholders, as opposed to returning the dollars back to the original bidders.

Unallocated	$0

	STAKEHOLDER						
	John (1.0)	Paul (1.0)	Georg (1.0)	Ringo (1.0)	Total bid	Dev cost	ROI
Change B	$3		$2		$5	3	1.7
Change C		$7	$2	$2	$11	7	1.6
Change E	$3	$2	$2	$1	$8	5	1.6
Change A					$0	2	0.0
Unspent	$4	$4	$4	$4			

Figure N-7. The unallocated dollars are divided among the stakeholders. They can add those dollars to existing bids or reallocate all of their allotted dollars.

Notice that Ringo doesn't get the $7 he originally bid on Change F to spend again; nor do John and George each get the $4 back, or Paul his $1, that they bid on Change D. Instead the total amount that was bid for changes D and F ($16) is divided equally amongst the four stakeholders. At the same time, however, the original bids for the remaining changes (B, C, E and A) remain in place, at least initially.

Once the available money is allocated, we then proceed as before. Each stakeholder bids on items in the product backlog using their unspent dollars. Each person can add his unspent dollars to the amount he bid before or he can choose to reallocate the dollars he has bid previously if his priorities have changed. For any bid-upon items that do not already have a development cost, a cost is calculated.

ROI is then calculated by dividing the total bid by the development cost. A new prioritised list is available for the next iteration. By redistributing development dollars and allowing the stakeholders to change previous bids, we are agile in response to changes in the stakeholders' priorities.

That's it! The process then repeats iteration by iteration. Dollars spent on each iteration are reallocated and re-bid.

Determining Stakeholder Weightings

The example above assumed equal weighting for each stakeholder. In a real-life project, some stakeholders will typically be less important than others. For example, stakeholders that only require a few reports from a system may be less important than the stakeholders that are responsible for data entry.

This can be handled in Priority Markets by assigning different weighting to the different stakeholders. This will affect the number of development dollars each stakeholder is allocated.

Let's modify our previous example with different weightings and then allocate our initial $40 in development dollars according to these values:

Unallocated	$0

	STAKEHOLDER				Total bid	Dev cost	ROI
	John (1.0)	Paul (1.0)	Georg (1.0)	Ringo (1.0)			
Change A						2	
Change B						3	
Change C						7	
Change D						4	
Change E						5	
Change F						2	
Unspent	$12	$10	$8	$10			

Figure N-8. Dollars are allocated based on stakeholder weighting for more accurate ROI results.

Here we see that, for this particular product, John is the most important stakeholder, George is the least and Paul and Ringo are considered equal. Their allocations, then, are based on their relative importance to the product. The weightings also reflect how much development effort is devoted to each stakeholder. In this example, John will receive 50% more development effort than George.

Determining who the stakeholders are and their individual weightings can be a politically challenging exercise. If the stakeholders cannot agree on a weighting among themselves, this decision should be made by the product owner, or senior product owner, if applicable. Whoever makes this decision must be someone sufficiently high in the organisational hierarchy.

In many regards, stakeholder weighting is analogous to a departmental budgeting process. An advantage of this approach is that management can make a single upfront decision about the relative priorities of the stakeholders for the product. This avoids them having to micromanage the relative merits of individual backlog items and empowers individual stakeholders with control of the priorities.

Benefits of Priority Markets

Priority Markets offer additional benefits to all project participants. Firstly, the method is scalable by the number of backlog items. In projects with hundreds of outstanding backlog items, Priority Markets allows the stakeholders and the development team to focus only on those changes that are of immediate relevance. This avoids the trap that many teams fall into of vigorously debating every item of a very long backlog. Items that do not have development dollars allocated to them stay in the backlog for consideration in future iterations.

Priority Markets also scales well with the number of stakeholders. Each stakeholder can bid independently of the others. A stakeholder can quantify the importance of their change request by bidding on them. This neatly avoids long discussions about why one backlog item may be more important than another. The process is also fair. If a stakeholder hasn't had any of their backlog items implemented in recent iterations they will have proportionally more dollars to spend in future iterations.

Furthermore, backlog prioritisation done through Priority Markets is an open process. At any time, each stakeholder can know the priorities of the other stakeholders and see how development dollars have been spent. Project priorities are openly set and transparent to all.

The Psychology of the Market

Monetising the prioritisation process allows some interesting behaviours to emerge.

Bargaining: Stakeholders can see one another's bids and adjust their bidding accordingly.

Trading: One stakeholder can "sell" their development dollars to another stakeholder for in-kind benefits.

Tactical voting: Based on others bids, a stakeholder may allocate more or fewer dollars to certain items.

Governmental intervention: When the free market generates priorities that are not in the strategic interests of the project, the product owner may step in and allocate additional dollars to a particular item. As with any free market, governmental intervention can have a number of negative consequences: extra dollars injected into the system reduces the relative value of other dollars, resulting in inflation; stakeholders may also feel disenfranchised by having their priorities overridden.

Conclusion

While there never will be a perfect solution to the difficult process of prioritisation, Pass the Cards and Priority Markets are two efficient and effective ways to mitigate any people-pleasing tendencies that might plague your negotiations. Both games give multiple stakeholders a chance to participate directly in a prioritisation process while mimimising standoffs and bickering.

In the next section, I'll discuss another common personality trait that can make negotiations difficult: perfectionism.

*Many people describe themselves as perfectionists
as if it were a badge of honour.*

Err and Excel

Good Product Owners avoid bad mistakes.
Great Product Owners make good mistakes quickly.

Hands up if you would happily describe yourself as a bit of a perfectionist.

Perfectionism is an interesting trait. The desire to be perfect is strong within the human population as a whole, so much so that many people describe themselves as perfectionists as if it were a badge of honour. In fact in a survey of over 200 people from my coaching practice, 65% of people rated their perfectionist trait as "slightly overdone" or "very overdone".

There are many good things about having high standards, especially in the world of product development. Customers don't want mediocrity, especially when competition is high and their choices are almost endless. Regulators won't tolerate a product that "sort of" meets compliance standards. So as a product owner, you need to be prepared to negotiate ruthlessly—with stakeholders pushing for extra features, with development teams looking to upgrade the technology, and sometimes with yourself when it comes to your desire for a perfect product.

> How much do you feel proud of the idea of being a perfectionist?

However, perfectionism has a dark side too. Many product owners who let their perfectionist trait get out of hand fall into the trap of trying to get the product perfect all at once, the first time. They are unable to make the tough calls required to deliver iteratively and are therefore unable to use feedback and learning to allow the perfect product to emerge over time.

Another trap that perfectionist product owners can fall into is not knowing when to stop the development of features or design. The temptation to just add a little extra here or there is very strong; but those "little bits here or there" quickly add up and can easily lead to significant launch delays, not to mention an unnecessarily cumbersome product to support.

> How has perfectionism hurt or hindered you personally or the products you have developed?

Perfection is an almost impossible goal, one that often daunts and stifles not just you but those around you as well. Great product owners understand how to manage their tendencies towards perfection while still achieving excellence.

Challenge Your Tendencies

As well as having a large impact on the product or service being developed, an out-of-balance perfectionism trait can have a large impact on the person too. People whose perfectionism trait has become a trap often focus exclusively on end results, are unable to enjoy the journey and, as a result, lose joy in their work. Setting high standards will often lead to great achievements, but if those standards become unrealistic then dissatisfaction, and quite often burnout too, are the likely results.

In his book, *Improv-ing Agile Teams: Using Constraints To Unlock Creativity*, Paul Goddard discusses the power of wearing hats when trying to think or act in new ways. He explains that "hats, masks, and even costumes can help people access their ideas more readily because they help individuals feel as if they are thinking like other people."

If you suspect that your perfectionist trait is potentially overdone then you might consider asking somebody on the product owner team to wear an imperfectionist hat: to adopt the persona of somebody whose explicit role is to challenge your perfectionism and always make a case for toning things down a little. This wouldn't be their full time job, of course, it may be as simple as bringing a certain hat (such as a panama hat) to meetings and asking someone to wear the imperfection panama and fill that role for this particular meeting.

Figure N-9: An imperfection panama hat may help you tackle your perfectionism

Or, even on your own, have an imperfection panama hat on hand. Put it on whenever you are thinking about prioritisation or the minimal feature set or any decision where you might let your perfectionist tendencies get away from you. This will allow you to get into the habit of negotiating with yourself.

Audit Your Influencers

The **Inner Board Room** technique is something that many people have found useful when managing their perfectionist tendencies. With this technique, you are encouraged to imagine that you have a board of directors governing your life. On this board are a range of people – some real, some imaginary – that have an influence on you and your decisions.

Those who find their perfectionist trait has become out of balance may find, by looking at who is currently on this imaginary board, that they are lacking an influential, ruthless or simplifying presence. When coaching product owners, I will often invite them to do an audit of the people who are influencing them and consciously choose who they want to be on their inner boardroom.

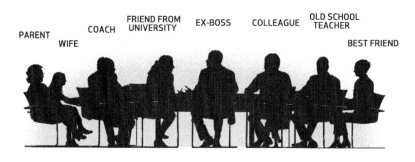

Fig N-10: Who currently holds a place in your Inner Boardroom?

Of course, a great Product Owner may have an actual group of people specifically gathered together in order to influence them –

The Product Owner Team. The Inner Boardroom technique can also be used to evaluate who is included or should be included on that team in order to help steer the product effectively between the competing extremes of perfection and over-simplification.

> Do you have the right voices and opinions on your product owner team to help you balance perfectionism and over-simplification?

Deliver the Next Perfect Slice

It's one thing to understand that the product can't be perfect; it's another to know how to effectively negotiate what exactly to deliver. Great product owners know that they can't afford to operate in an "all or nothing" mindset and instead harness the opportunities available to them in an empirical approach such as Scrum to focus on "continual excellence" rather than perfection.

In the story that opens this section, Karen rightly surrounded herself with subject matter experts to help her make the tough decisions. When Jamie described a compromise product that included most of the stakeholder requirements, Karen was tempted to choose the easy solution. But Karen was also experienced enough to know that, though the stakeholder arguments and the data may seem conflicting, contradictory, and overwhelming at times, she needed to choose only the features that were best for the overall product.

Karen ultimately chose a strategic – and agile – approach to incremental value delivery. She decided to pick apart the various aspects of the solution that Jamie created and prioritise them ruthlessly in order to deliver more focused value sooner rather than aim for a bigger delivery later. This can be hard to do for many product owners who see the value in all of the important requests and potential options in front of them. The key here is to define perfection in terms that are helpful: Deliver a perfect slice of the product rather than a perfect complete product.

 What does a perfect slice of your product look like?

The great product owners would rather "delight" a smaller audience than "barely satisfy" a larger group. As such, they tighten the product's focus, which results in a smaller development effort and a cheaper—and quicker—product release. It may well be that, for this initial product, the product owner discovers they have chosen the wrong features or left out desired features. Rather than consider this a mistake—great product owners know that they have spent a minimal amount of money to learn valuable information.

Please don't misunderstand. I'm not saying that taking the time to consult many experts and to think things through is a bad idea. It's not! Avoiding the kinds of mistakes caused by rushing, ignoring the data, or failing to take key factors into consideration is a good thing. But great product owners also understand that combining a smaller development effort with faster feedback ultimately allows them to shift their focus more rapidly (and with more accuracy) to the next target and dedicate their efforts in that direction.

Make Good Mistakes

The desire to be perfect has a huge impact on our ability to get started and make progress. While a product owner should set a high standard for the product they are bringing to market and push relentlessly to make it as good as it can possibly be, the best product owners know how to recognize the signs of excess and can negotiate fiercely in order to simplify the product.

The terms Minimal Viable Product (MVP) and Lean Startup have evolved to try to solidify the need for product managers to focus solely on the bare essentials. The Pareto principle (also known as the 80:20 rule) states that roughly 80% of the value comes from 20% of the effort—it has been a guiding rule of thumb for many domains since 1896.

Despite knowing this, we seem to find it inherently difficult to simplify and deliver something imperfect. Economics writer Tim Harford, in his TED Talk *"Trial, Error and the God Complex"*, makes the case for more extensive use of trial and error in all walks of life, including product development. He acknowledges how difficult this is, though, by citing Goro Shimura who, when reflecting on his friend Yutaka Taniyama's life, said, "He made a lot of mistakes. But he made mistakes in a good direction. I tried to imitate him. But I've realised that it's very difficult to make good mistakes."

Can you identify some beneficial mistakes you have made?

What mistakes might be worth making now?

Early on in my career, the company I worked for experienced this same difficulty with making mistakes. Our culture included the desire to be "right first time." So we would plan, plan, and plan again in the hopes of making sure that when we eventually got around to doing something, it would be correct. Over the years, as projects and technology grew more complicated, it became harder and harder to achieve our "right first time" goal, regardless of how long we spent trying to work things out. Meanwhile our competitors were getting their products to market in less time than it took us to plan ours. Times had changed.

At what point does "right first time" become "wrong too late"?

How close are you coming to that point?

Another problem that we had was that, even after all of our meticulous planning, we very often ended up delivering the wrong product. Technically it was correct because we had delivered the requirements that had been agreed up front but because so much had changed over the course of the project (with regards to technology and understanding) what we delivered ended up being obsolete. We called these projects technical successes because technically they were a success: we had delivered the pre-defined requirements on time and within budget. In reality, however, these projects were failures because they provided little to no value to our customers.

We began to understand that our definition of "right first time" had to change. And it took someone very senior within the organisation to go on record and say so. He held an all-hands call (a phone call where every member of the organisation was expected to join) and explained that our definition of failure was changing. From now on, he said, failure was not to be feared; failure was an acceptable outcome so long as we failed quickly, cheaply, and that we didn't fail the same way twice. This freed us to minimise our plans and maximise our production—and to be more creative and innovative in our approach to problem solving.

Good mistakes, therefore, are ones that:

- Are made in good faith, in the pursuit of doing the right thing for the product rather than the easy decision or the fear of making the wrong decision.
- Allow us to find out what works and what doesn't work quickly and cheaply.
- Keep as many options open to us as possible for as long as possible.
- Reduce the risks in the project early.

Product owners need to be comfortable making good mistakes, and to encourage development teams to make them too.

Add Dimension with Story Mapping

One way to make mistakes more palatable is to identify and mitigate (if not remove) risk from the product as early as possible. The best way to do this is to ruthlessly prioritise and structure the product backlog—the prioritised list of user needs that continually evolves as knowledge is gained and conditions change. By always having a stack-ranked list of work product owners can ensure that the development team is always working on the most valuable items while mitigating the wasted effort of detailing out everything in advance. However, more and more of the great product owners tend to display the needs of the product in two dimensions (rather than just a one-dimensional product backlog) through what has become known as a story map.

Story mapping most likely evolved as a common-sense response to the limitations of a one-dimensional list of work. Indeed teams were using something very similar to this approach when I was working at BT back in 2001. However, I am going to attribute it to the first person I saw to write about this as a way of working—*Jeff Patton*. To his credit, rather than claim its invention, he notes that other people likely came up with the same approach.

When creating a story map, start with a large wall, table, floor, screen (or whatever other medium you are choosing to create your map). Whatever you choose needs to be a big enough whiteboard or wall to hold the resulting story map! Begin by listing the **user activities** as a horizontal row at the top of the map. Jeff describes user activities as "sort of a big thing that people do – something that has lots of steps, and doesn't always have a precise workflow." For me, I would consider these the main functional areas of the product or service being designed. Other product owners more familiar with the concept of **user stories** may choose to use the term **theme** or **epic** perhaps.

These user activities are laid out in sequential order of how a user would typically interact with them, with earlier interactions on the left and later interactions on the right. For example, on an online shopping site I typically search for a product, then add it to my wish list or basket, then check out. My user activities from left to right would be "search for a product", "add to basket", and "check out".Perfectionists may struggle with working out a clear, linear order. If you find yourself unable to choose, remember that this does not have to be a perfect representation of all possible scenarios, merely good enough to enable you to plan.

Underneath each of these activities would be what Jeff calls **user tasks**—smaller items of functionality that contribute towards achieving the overall activity above—you might refer to these elements as **user stories**. Again these would be listed in order, with the highest priority tasks being nearer the top than those at the bottom. For example, under the user activity "search for a product", you might have user tasks such as "search by name", "search previously ordered products" and "search related products".

Finally, below each **user task**, list the subtasks or task details. To continue with the previous example, user task "search previously ordered products" would likely have **task details** such as "store previously ordered products", "display previously ordered products" and perhaps "filter previously ordered products".

A standard story map structure might look something like this:

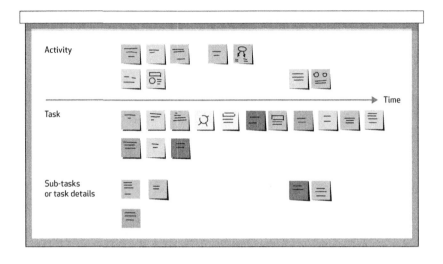

Figure N-11: A story map allows you to visualise the product across multiple dimensions.

This multi-dimensional approach gives greater visibility of the bigger picture for all stakeholders. It also helps a product owner better visualise how to slice the product into valuable releases because it takes into account all the necessary aspects of the product rather than just being a virtual stack of items that you choose one-by-one in a priority manner.

Conclusion

Agile product owners realise that they will rarely have the luxury of achieving perfection. Great product owners embrace this fact by finding ways to make cheap and early mistakes to learn more about the product as quickly as possible. As paradoxical as this may seem, **great product owners err in order to excel**.

As we discussed earlier, being decisive and ruthless are common characteristics of successful product owners. However, a product owner also must be open to negotiation with multiple stakeholders in order to create a well-rounded product. Great product owners know, therefore, that they must also be prepared to negotiate, because they are likely to have to make some kind of trade-offs, usually over functionality or time or both.

Be DRIVEN to Be Great

Good product owners know how to use
agile tools and artefacts.
Great product owners are DRIVEN to develop
their subtle, softer skills.

Throughout this book, I have demonstrated ways in which good product owners can work towards becoming great in order to be successful in a world where customer needs, technology and market conditions change so rapidly. Great product owners are DRIVEN: decisive, ruthless, informed, versatile, empowering and negotiable. Great product owners embrace unpredictability in part by being **decisive**. They know the importance of moving forward in spite of any perfectionist tendencies but also recognise the power of delaying decisions until the last responsible moment. As such, they gather as much data as possible while simultaneously reducing the cost of wrong decisions. They are also humble enough to involve others in the decision making process to improve the quality and timeliness of those decisions, to increase engagement, and also to allow them to focus their time on the most important issues.

Being decisive is one of many areas where a product owner needs to be **ruthless** at times. In order to build a great product, great product owners prioritise ruthlessly. It is often impossible to deliver everything and certainly impossible to deliver everything all at once; so great product owners work tirelessly to target their efforts on the absolutely critical areas. To do this successfully, they often have to battle their tendencies to want to please others and focus instead on what is best for the product.

Great product owners are prepared to take calculated gambles in uncertain environments but are also always prepared to be ruthless about cutting their losses should the empirical data they are collecting indicate that the return on the investment simply isn't there. This is no easy task as this will involve disappointing stakeholders or letting go of one's own ideas but thinking strategically and objectively while practicing a little mindfulness can make this side of the role a little easier.

The empirical data that product owners are collecting through an iterative, incremental development process such as Scrum will also help them become more **informed** and, as such, more effective. As well as gathering as much information as possible by researching the market, the users, the technology, and the product space, great product owners realise that they most likely will have to act with incomplete information and some degree of uncertainty.

Great product owners also work at becoming informed about themselves, their cognitive biases and where they have gaps in their understanding. They know that, as well as being able to answer the team's questions, they must be willing to tap the collective knowledge of the team by asking curious, humble, illuminative, limitless and direct questions.

Knowing when to answer questions and when to ask questions is a good example of a DRIVEN product owner being **versatile**. There is a lot to be said for a product owner providing clarity and stability to a team that is operating in an environment of uncertainty and change. However, the best product owners never let their reliability become rigidity. They adapt their leadership style based on the circumstances, building rapport with the team and stakeholders while maintaining the necessary professionalism to have crucial conversations where necessary.

Great product owners are also naturally versatile when it comes to the product, being able to create and articulate a clear and compelling vision for the product to be developed and staying true to that vision as long as it holds up. They will also be rigorous in fine-tuning that vision when new information comes to light during the empirical product development process.

The product owner is expected to be the owner of the vision for the product and to generate enthusiasm, support and buy-in for that vision then manage the product backlog and the stakeholders in order to maximise return on investment while delivering that product. They are therefore expected to provide a clear leadership role. This doesn't always have to be leading from the front however. Great product owners are **empowering**; they strive to involve and engage the development team, working with them as collaborative partners. They get past any fears they may have about trust by hiring well, supporting individual and team development, and developing a respectful and open relationship with the team.

While working with the development team, great product owners also create and evolve strategies that empower and motivate the development team to be proactive, creative and innovative; for example, by giving them problems to solve (or telling them stories they can create) rather than specific requirements to implement.

Finally, all great product owners know they need to be **negotiable** in order to be successful. It is rarely possible to please everyone and still create the best possible product. It is imperative therefore to be able to negotiate amongst all the stakeholders for the good of the product. Great product owners remember that the delivered product will not be perfect either, so they negotiate the features, focusing on the next perfect "slice" of the product to be delivered incrementally.

Iterative, incremental product development will inevitably involve mistakes. Great product owners negotiate risk by avoiding bad mistakes while also tackling their inner perfectionist by embracing the power of making good mistakes early (or maximising learning as it might better be known).

Being an agile product owner is a tough job but a highly rewarding one. There are many tools and artefacts available to make the practical side of the job slightly easier but, no matter what product or service we are building, the process is inevitably going to involve people. Therefore, the biggest difference between the good product owners and the great product owners is how much they have grasped the subtler, softer, more people-focussed characteristics required to master the role.

I hope this book has inspired you to become a more DRIVEN product owner.

Appendix

What Is Scrum?

Scrum is an agile framework, which means it falls under the larger umbrella of the agile manifesto and therefore shares the values and principles stated in the agile manifesto. The aim of Scrum is to provide a framework for being agile in product development or on project work. Using Scrum, discrete pieces of work are built within a constraint of either a fixed end-date or (sometimes) a fixed scope. Scrum is usually most useful in environments of complexity, uncertainty and/or change volatility.

Scrum defines three roles for its projects: a product owner, a Scrum-master, and a development team. Together, these three roles make up the Scrum team. In very broad terms, the product owner determines what will be built, the development team decides how to build it, and the ScrumMaster ensures that the development team and product owner are able to do these things.

The Scrum framework begins with the product owner establishing a vision for the product or project—a reason for this piece of work to exist and attract funding. Scrum is an empirical or heuristic framework; as such the requirements for the project are expected to emerge over the course of the project. Because of this the goal of the project is vitally important because the ultimate success of the project will be judged not by whether the requirements were met but whether the vision was achieved.

That is not to say that there are no requirements in Scrum—there are, and they are captured in what Scrum calls a product backlog.

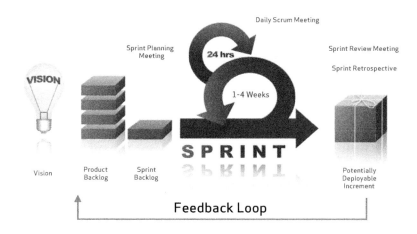

The product backlog is ever changing but, at all times, is kept in priority order by the product owner and estimated by the development team, so that a rolling plan of work can be assessed. Most Scrum teams will begin by creating a release plan to gain an initial view of the viability of the project. A release plan will take the prioritised and estimated product backlog and provide a rough answer to either "how long will this amount of product backlog take?" or "how much of our product backlog can we expect by this date?"

Regardless of whether the team creates a release plan, all Scrum teams will go through sprint planning. A sprint is a short timebox, typically one to four weeks, in which the team agrees to produce a potentially shippable product increment from a certain set of product backlog items. A sprint planning session involves the self-organising development team determining which product backlog items they feel able to commit to for the current sprint and devising a plan for how they intend to deliver them.

During the sprint, the development team will work towards this sprint commitment. Scrum provides two specific tools to help the team manage their work: the daily scrum and the sprint burndown. The daily scrum is a short, 15-minute, status-sharing and re-planning meeting for the members of the development team. The sprint burndown is a very simple graph of planned versus outstanding work for the sprint.

At the end of the sprint, Scrum calls for an open-invite meeting called the sprint review. During the sprint review, the Scrum team gets the opportunity to formally review the deliveries from the sprint, often with other project stakeholders who aren't involved on a daily basis. This is also when the product owner gets an opportunity to use the feedback from the stakeholders in order to change the direction of the product and when the release plan is updated based on the latest empirical data. The sprint review is followed by a sprint retrospective, where the development team gets the opportunity to evaluate the previous sprint and identify opportunities to optimise and/or change their process to improve.

Acknowledgements

There have been many people who have helped me with this book and I like to think that I have thanked them all personally but it is also important that their contributions are recorded properly.

Firstly, Rebecca Traeger has been more than an editor on this project. She has been a sounding board, a provocateur and instigator at times. Without her efforts, during very difficult circumstances, this book would not have made it and I am very grateful to her.

Secondly, the artwork by Ole Størksen once again adds a great dimension to the text. Ole has yet again gone above and beyond and I personally love the hand-drawn illustrations in this book and I am very grateful to him.

As the book evolved over the two years I spent writing it, I interviewed many people for different aspects. They were all generous with their time and the sharing of their wisdom and opinions. In the end, largely because the structure of the book ended up very different to how I initially envisaged it, many of those contributions didn't make their way explicitly into the final version. However, these interviews were incredibly valuable and I still appreciate the time they took out of their lives to speak to me. As great product owners, they all appreciate the need to make some ruthless decisions at times!

Thank you to Fiona McLaren who worked with me on the chapter that told the story of product ownership at Made by Many. I really liked that fact that this book was not simply a collection of my experiences and adding a story that offered that independent air while also touching on the extra dimension of being a product owner at an agency adds something great to the book and I'm grateful to her for that.

I had many people review my work as I was writing and I am grateful to all of them. I want to single out Roman Pichler, Jeff Sutherland for their guidance, friendship and forewords as well as Paul Goddard and Roger Malvern who, as has been the case for 20 years, again went above and beyond in both their support and feedback.

Jess Larmont has also been a great help to me in bringing everything together and getting my message out to the world, for which I am very grateful.

And lastly, my family who reacted to my "I think I might write another book" with understanding and support rather than "Oh no…but you promised…" which they would have been entitled to.

And if you are reading this then I am grateful to you for buying, borrowing or just somehow getting your hands on it.

References

DECISIVE

Ackermann, F., & Eden, C. (2011). Strategic Management of Stakeholders: Theory and Practice. Long Range Planning, 44(3), 179-196. doi:10.1016/j.lrp.2010.08.001

Harford, T. (n.d.). Trial, error and the God complex. Retrieved January 02, 2017, from https://www.ted.com/talks/tim_harford?language=e

Iyengar, S. S., & Lepper, M. R. (2000). When choice is demotivating: Can one desire too much of a good thing? Journal of Personality and Social Psychology,79(6), 995-1006. doi:10.1037//0022-3514.79.6.995

Partnoy, F. (n.d.). Waiting Game: What Tennis Teaches Us. Retrieved June 22, 2012, from http://www.ft.com/cms/s/2/4551e9ee-b9fd-11e1-937b-00144feabdc0.html/

Poppendieck, M., & Poppendieck, T. D. (2003). Lean software development: an agile toolkit. Boston, MA: Addison-Wesley.

Reed, L. W., & Friedman, M. (1999). I, pencil: my family tree as told to Leonard E. Read. Irvington-on-Hudson: Foundation for Economic Education. http://www.econlib.org/library/Essays/rdPncl1.html/

Scotland, K. (2010, April 06). Defining the Last Responsible MomentAvailAgility. Retrieved January 02, 2017, from http://availagility.co.uk/2010/04/06/defining-the-last-responsible-moment/

Warrell, M. (2014, April 03). Afraid Of Being 'Found Out?' How To Overcome Impostor Syndrome. Retrieved January 02, 2017, from http://www.forbes.com/sites/margiewarrell/2014/04/03/impostor-syndrome/#3f544e5ceb9d

Watts, G., & Morgan, K. (2015). The Coach's Casebook: Mastering the Twelve Traits That Trap Us. Cheltenham: Inspect & Adapt Ltd.

RUTHLESS

Covey, S. R. (1989). The Seven Habits of Highly Effective People: restoring the character ethic. New York: Simon and Schuster.

Sunk Cost Fallacy, Wikipedia, https://en.wikipedia.org/wiki/Sunk_cost#Loss_aversion_and_the_sunk_cost_fallacy

INFORMED

Cipriano, M., "The Power of Priors: How Confirmation Bias Impacts Market Prices", The Journal of Prediction Markets Vol 8, No 3 (2014)

Kano, Noriaki; Nobuhiku Seraku; Fumio Takahashi; Shinichi Tsuji (April 1984). "Attractive quality and must-be quality". Journal of the Japanese Society for Quality Control (in Japanese). 14 (2): 39–48.

Covey, S. R. (1989). The Seven Habits of Highly Effective People: restoring the character ethic. New York: Simon and Schuster.

VERSATILE

Goleman, D., Boyatzis, R. E., & McKee, A. (2002). Primal leadership: realizing the power of emotional intelligence. Boston, MA: Harvard Business School Press.

Patterson, K., Grenny, J., McMillan, R., & Switzler, A. (2002). Crucial Conversations: tools for talking when stakes are high. New York: McGraw-Hill.

We like challenges. (n.d.). Retrieved January 02, 2017, from https://madebymany.com/about

Covey, S. R. (1989). The Seven Habits of Highly Effective People: restoring the character ethic. New York: Simon and Schuster.

Bain & Company: Net Promoter System - Net Promoter System Home. (n.d.). Retrieved January 02, 2017, from http://netpromotersystem.com/

Online. (n.d.). Retrieved January 02, 2017, from http://www.mccarthyshow.com/online

EMPOWERING

Beck, K. et al (2001). Principles behind the Agile Manifesto. Retrieved January 02, 2017, from http://agilemanifesto.org/principles.html

User Stories. (n.d.). Retrieved January 02, 2017, from https://www.agilealliance.org/glossary/user-stories/

Cooper, A. (1999). The inmates are running the asylum: why high-tech products drive us crazy and how to restore the sanity. Indianapolis, IN: Sams.

Goddard, P. (2015). Improv-ing agile teams. Amazon Createspace.

Fear of Public Speaking Statistics. (n.d.). Retrieved January 02, 2017, from http://www.statisticbrain.com/fear-of-public-speaking-statistics/

Watts, G., & Goddard, P. (2012, October 23). Story Spines. Retrieved January 02, 2017, from http://tastycupcakes.org/2012/10/story-spines/

NEGOTIABLE

Watts, G., & Morgan, K. (2015). The Coach's Casebook: Mastering the Twelve Traits That Trap Us. Cheltenham: Inspect & Adapt Ltd.

Tabaka, J. (2006). Collaboration explained: facilitation skills for software project leaders. Upper Saddle River, NJ: Addison-Wesley.

Watts, G., & Haines, J. (2009, February). Priority Markets. Retrieved January 2, 2017, from https://www.scrumalliance.org/community/articles/2009/february/priority-markets

Goddard, P. (2015). Improv-ing agile teams. Amazon Createspace.

Harford, T. (n.d.). Trial, error and the God complex.
Retrieved January 02, 2017, from https://www.ted.com/talks/
tim_harford?language=e

Patton, J. (n.d.). The New Backlog. Retrieved October, 2016, from
http://www.agileproductdesign.com/blog/the_new_backlog.html

Index

A

B

C

D

Q

R

S

Printed in Great Britain
by Amazon

35707066R00165